The Great Animated Movies

MARK MCPHERSON

ISBN-13: 978-1530191505
ISBN-10: 1530191505

FOR MOM AND DAD

CONTENTS

INTRODUCTION

Animation is a medium of limitless potential and imagination that need not constrict to one demographic or style. It was always appealing to me in that I never placed animation in the box of children's toys to be stored away with age. It wasn't that hard a task considering the boom in more independent, foreign and adult animated films in recent years. There's even a presence of more adult-targeted animation on television with *The Simpsons*, *Family Guy* and *South Park*, all of which have been airing on television for over a decade. Animation is even taken seriously at both the box office and the Academy Awards as one of the few types of films that can be both a blockbuster and an award winner.

So why does it still feel as though this stigma of animation only being a distraction for children is still present? It could be that most animation presented commercially comes in the form of family entertainment. It could be the lack of marketing for the smaller, more challenging animated films that are beginning to grow in numbers. Whatever the reason, animated films deserve to be seen as so much more.

I set out to write this book to provide a spotlight to lesser known animated films, but also brighter exposure on animated films that have been labeled as little more than children's entertainment. *Finding Nemo* was more than just a cute tale about fish and *Fritz the Cat* was not just an exercise in animating for an X rating. There was an old joke in the hallways of junior high school that cartoons only came in two categories: *PokeMon* and pornography. This implied that animation was either meant to sell toys or titillate and shock the viewer. This book is all about that gray area in between that needs to be recognized as animation with a true sense of great filmmaking.

This is not an all-inclusive book of animated films based on them being either "cute" or "adult". Since animation has become a big business at the cinema, I will often see bland productions that appear more manufactured for simple laughs and toy campaigns than artistic displays of the medium. By that same token, I have also seen animated films that aim to be crude and adult for the sake of being just that without anything meaningful to say. The entries in this book are animated films that have resonated well over time with just as much story and character as stunning visuals.

Though I have seen many of the films in this book repeatedly over the years, I made a point to rewatch every title for writing this book. Watching these films again has brought back many fond memories from my childhood, teenage and college years. I recall spending much of my teen years begging my parents to take me downtown to view the latest animation festivals and animated films that were not commercial enough for the local theaters. College was a unique time when I discovered many of the more the adult animated films in class and among viewing groups. I have never forgotten these experiences and these films have remained etched in my mind for the longest time.

The films presented in this book are what I consider to be classics of the medium. Since I based most of these essays on the impact these films have over time, I set a minimum of at least five years since theatrical release. So if you're looking for recent animated films such as *Inside Out* or *The Peanuts Movie*, I'm sorry to say you won't find them in this book (perhaps in a future edition).

As if I didn't need another reason to write this book, The Hollywood Reporter published some rather shocking interviews from anonymous voters of the Academy Awards and how they vote for Best Animated Feature. Most of the voters either abstained or went with the film their kids found the most entertaining. One particular voter was so steamed that *The Lego Movie* wasn't nominated that the voter referred to the nominations of the Japanese *The Tale of Princess Kaguya* and the Irish *Song of the Sea* as "obscure freakin' Chinese f**kin' things that nobody ever freakin' saw."

My hope is that this book will inspire others to look at such familiar animated films with a different eye and discover other gems they never knew existed. Perhaps then some of the lesser known animated films won't be seen as obscure and not all of them as Chinese.

AKIRA

Japanese animation started gaining an American cult following in the 1980's, but it was *AKIRA* (1988) that sparked the explosion of a larger following and exposed many Americans to the medium's full potential. Though relegated to arthouse cinemas for its limited theatrical debut, the film soon grew in popularity that it became a cult hit on home video and a staple of Japanese animation enthusiasts. The film featured hand-drawn animation quality that could easily go toe-to-toe with the Disney juggernauts. This was animation being used not for cute animals and bouncy musical numbers, but for violent motorcycle chases across a neon metropolis and psychic showdowns amid epic levels of destruction.

How such a project came together sounds almost like a dream project come true. Katsuhiro Otomo was provided one of the finest offers for adapting his comic book series into a feature film, given total creative control acting as the film's director. The project had a massive budget of ¥1,100,000,000 pooled together from various sponsors that included Kodansha, Toho and the Laserdisc Corporation among others. This collaboration of producers was known as The AKIRA Committee.

The final results were astounding. From its opening shot of Neo Tokyo being silently consumed by light to the final perplexing shots of the cosmos, there is never a dull moment or bland visual on screen. The streets of Neo Tokyo boom with colorfully commercial displays of lights and holograms that make *Blade Runner*'s towering Los Angeles seem minute by comparison. Motorcycles zoom through the dirty city streets so fast they leave small streaks of lights behind them. Rival gangs clash in high-speed rumbles where cyclists are thrown through windows, cracked in the head by crowbars and brutally crushed by the force of passing bikes. And that's just the first ten minutes.

The script is essentially an epic revenge story with the mysteries of the universe mixed in for good measure. Tetsuo is the runt of a metropolis motorcycle gang led by the brotherly Kaneda. He desperately wants to prove himself as a tough guy, but hasn't quite reached that level and is looked down on by his fellow gang members. An unfortunate crash leaves Tetsuo captured by the government who suspect he has superpowers related to a cataclysmic disaster that transformed regular Tokyo into Neo-Tokyo. He shares a ward with similar individuals of such powers that appear in elderly-looking children. Tetsuo's abilities have the scientists impressed, the military frightened and his gang longing to rescue their comrade.

But after the initial shock to Tetsuo's brain being haunted and taunted by the mysterious boy AKIRA, he discovers how to use his powers and is ready to bring havoc on the world he feels has wronged him. With a mere thought, he splatters the hospital security forces into the walls. The other psychic children attempt to stop him, but to no avail. Cackling and furious, Tetsuo has become an unstoppable monster. He's far more infatuated with his power than anything else in life. The shrimp becomes a whale and desires to eat the entire ocean.

Tetsuo's rampage is a magnificent and detailed display of chilling carnage. He walks the streets in a red cape, seen by members of cults as the coming of AKIRA that they perceive as some sort of messiah. They follow him through the streets as he destroys the military forces trying to stop him. While crossing a bridge to discover the secret resting place of AKIRA, Tetsuo's path is halted by soldiers with laser weaponry and tanks. He responds by lifting up sections of the bridge, forcing everybody and everything on it to topple into the water below. A tank sinks off a cliff of concrete onto its muzzle causing an explosion. Scores of soldiers and followers cling hopelessly to the bridge as they descend. A cult leader clings to one of his members, but is forced downward as flaming wreckage knocks off the bridge.

It's the little details that make *AKIRA* such a striking animated film. There are massive crowd shots where nearly every character seems to be alive and active. Several night shots of the city involve high-level protests where rebels wave flags and turn over cars as riot control fires tear gas wildly for dispersal. There's a brief shot where one officer spots a protester coughing his way out of the cloud of gas. The officer responds by shooting him point-blank in the chest with a gas canister.

While *AKIRA* seems to mostly be a disaster picture with large structures being decimated at every turn, it's far more than just meaningless destruction with its additional elements of graphic horror. When people are killed in these violent acts of explosions and toppling buildings, we see all the blood and death whereas most directors would keep such displays off-screen for a PG-13 rating. Tetsuo's powers are portrayed as unstably dangerous as when he attacks the doctors who try to make him go back to his room. Rather than shove them away with his psychic powers, he smashes their bodies into the ceiling so hard they appear more as bloody wallpaper than human beings.

The city of Neo-Tokyo represents a society that has grown so towering that it is toppling over on itself. Every piece of architecture is monstrously oversized from an outdoor bridge looming several flights above the city streets to the largest beer can advertisement perched on a skyscraper. Even a chase through the sewage system appears in an extraordinarily large location. An enormous Olympic stadium, still being built as dwindling funds go into its construction, serves as the perfect platform for the grand finale. It's excess that begs to be torn down by the angst youth who deface it with graffiti and demolish it with rebellion.

Though there are plenty of brutal deaths to be had, there are also some much more subtle ones. A greedy politician attempts to flee down an alley with a bloated briefcase of documents, but his heart condition leaves him clutching his chest. He desperately opens his bottle of pills, but cannot swallow the many that he's forced into his mouth. As the briefcase documents scatter in the wind, the politician collapses in an alley. Behind him is a rebel secret agent he shot prior that stumbles forward just a few steps more to witness the riots in the streets. He leans against a wall and slowly drifts off into death.

As Tetsuo's power grows unstable, he starts becoming less human. His damaged arm which he repairs with artificial materials becomes a festering mess of pulsating flesh. Tetsuo's body becomes completely unstable as he transforms into a massive blob of mutating tissue seeming to form appendages and orifices at will. It's easily one of the most disgusting sights I've ever seen in an animated film, especially when he traps a character in between the pockets of his expanding flesh and crushes them to death in a bloody mess. With so much detail and grossness, it's almost a tribute to John Carpenter's barf-bag worthy effects for *The Thing*.

With so much disturbing and dark imagery present on screen, *AKIRA* is not an easy film to watch for first-time viewers. I first saw the film when I was twelve and it left me uneasy and queasy (and not just for the visual body horror). But I came back to it a few days later and found myself infatuated with all its intensity. I started noticing more detail in every shot and managed to find something new with each viewing. Having seen the film at least a dozen times since, it's still as mesmerizing with each watch.

The foremost element that remained in my brain after the initial viewing was the hauntingly catchy soundtrack by Shoji Yamashiro. His conduction makes wonderful use of powerful drums and a versatile choir. The opening shots are mostly silent with small beats of loud drums echoing off into the distance. The first act motorcycle chase turns up the pace of the drums as the choir goes from a Gregorian monk tone to that of a punk rock vibe. When the evil Klown biker gang is introduced, the voices take center stage using heavy breathing to convey a sense of danger and speed.

AKIRA was one of the trickiest anime films to dub over into English. The majority of Japanese animation tends to rely on simple mouth flaps as opposed to animated lips that form the correct shape for every word spoken. This is due to the limited budget and time of a production in which animation is assembled ahead of the dialogue. That was not the case with *AKIRA* as the mouths were animated to the exact phrasing of the Japanese dialogue. If there was a "U" in the dialogue, the mouth would form a "U" position of the lips and so on. This caused fundamental problems with the two times *AKIRA* was dubbed by English voice actors.

The first dub by Streamline Pictures in 1989 focused less on accuracy and more on acting. The actors do their best to match the lips as much as possible, but there are some scenes they just can't quite keep up with. There is a scene in a conference room where a frustrated board member is buzzing in his chair, slapping the table and becoming irritated as he rattles off dialogue incredibly fast. The English voice actor could simply not keep up with this character and his seemingly endless string of dialogue. The English dub featured the voice actor reading the dialogue naturally and leaving that awkward silence when the English script is too short to cover the entire movement of the lips. It looks very off.

However, the English director on that script knew that you can't rattle off dialogue that fast or you end up with the stereotypical style of kung-fu dubbing. This occurs when there is far too much dialogue in a short period of time that actors have to read off the lines with rapid speed to keep up, as if every character has to go to the bathroom between sentences. Those who have seen the English dubbing of *Speed Racer* are familiar with this style of direction. Such direction maintains better accuracy, but leaves much to be desired in the acting. This is the crux of the 2001 dub by Pioneer in which characters speak far too quickly and lose that sense of character the Streamline dub possessed. Both are available on the current Blu-ray release by FUNimation so you can compare and contrast for yourself.

Since the success of the film, Otomo became a name synonymous with grand-scale disasters in anime films. While working on his next project *Steamboy* (2004), he served as animation supervisor for *Spriggan* (1998) and the screenwriter for *Metropolis* (2001). You can see his influence in those pictures as massive structures crush crowded city streets. Otomo's presence is there in that he wants such sights to appear with lots of detail. It isn't enough that a building topples over; Otomo wants us to see everyone caught in the carnage to let us know that it isn't just destruction without consequences. Both *Spriggan* and *Metropolis* were films I caught on the big screen which is the only way to catch all the little details of these destructive sequences.

Years after my initial wonderment of Japanese animation had subsided, *AKIRA* still holds up. It's just as exciting, challenging, disturbing and telling as the day I rented it on VHS from the video store. The tremendous ambition continues to shine through with a lasting impression of ruthless storytelling and animation – it has the same Disney level of spectacle, but with a wildly violent and dystopian kick.

ALADDIN

If you talk to anybody who grew up watching Disney's animated films of the early 1990's, you'll most likely find that none of them will be able to name the voice actor of Ariel from *The Little Mermaid* or the beast from *Beauty and the Beast*. But I guarantee they'll all be able to name Robin Williams as the voice of the genie from *Aladdin* (1992).

It wasn't merely a case of him being a recognizable comedic talent as much as it was his voice performance being one of the most memorable in all of animation. No role was more perfect for an actor such as Williams considering that directors Ron Clements and John Musker had him in mind when conceiving the character of Genie. To convince Williams that he was a great fit for such a role, animator Eric Goldberg lifted audio from one of Williams' stand-up routines and animated Genie around the dialogue. The drawings of Genie growing multiple heads to illustrate schizophrenia made Williams laugh and agree to voice the character.

His performance is noteworthy in that it broke from the usual method of voice recording. Rather than read straight from the script, Williams was given a general description of scenes and was then let loose on the microphone. He unleashed his manic mode of comedic zingers and impersonations with his fast timing and quick wit. For his additional role as a traveling trader, Williams was given a table of props and put all his humorous improv talents to work while being recorded. When the audio was handed over to the animators, it was less a case of which readings were the best takes as it was a matter of which ones were the funniest.

When the plucky thief Aladdin first awakens Genie from his magical lamp, the blue and mystical being rises in a smoky blast that reveals his towering presence. His mighty roar upon being released is followed by rubbing his neck and commenting on the cramped living quarters of a magic lamp. 10,000 years in such a small space probably would put a cramp on the neck. Genie then proceeds to introduce himself and explain his powers in the form of both extravagant musical numbers and impressive celebrity impersonations. Every scene where he is present is dominated by his ability to chew scenery. It was that frantic level of comedic power that managed to elevate this animated adaptation of *One Thousand and One Nights* into something more.

Though Williams stole the show for his powerful performance, there are some noteworthy characters that stick out as well. The second most recognizable voice from the cast is the always vocal comedian Gilbert Gottfried, voicing the talking parrot Iago. Gottfried isn't as fast as Williams, but he's just as loud the way he dominates every scene when appearing on the shoulder of his evil master Jafar. He was built for that character the way his crass and nasally tone lends itself to the voice of a parrot constantly squawking and complaining. Iago was originally supposed to be a more collected character while Jafar was the one with a short fuse. I think most will agree the swap in character was a good choice.

But some characters didn't even need to have a voice to stick out as with the sentient character of the magic carpet. With its intricate surface design rendered in computer animation, the faceless creation was able to interact fluidly with all the characters while maintaining the tapestry of an Egyptian pattern. He's able to express a surprising amount of emotion for being a flat surface with only corner tassels to work with as appendages.

The magic carpet became an essential character to the story even after his big CGI set piece of helping Aladdin escape a tidal wave of lava. Credit for the character should be given to animator Randy Cartwright who kept folding paper as reference to create a sense of realism and character. The results speak for themselves as an inanimate object displays a wide range of emotions. When the carpet is sad, he folds over on himself and slowly sulks from side to side. When the carpet is shocked, he extends his corners outward. He's an easily readable character for one that has no dialogue, face or limbs.

It may not say much about our lead protagonists when the side characters have so many interesting qualities, but they're not too shabby either. The thief boy Aladdin is plucky, crafty and has a good heart. After risking his life to steal a loaf of bread, he tosses it to some doe-eyed, homeless orphans. Within the same scene, he also saves them from a snobby prince who nearly tramples them. His wit matches his heart and he is even directly referred to by legend as a diamond in the rough. He's a likable enough lad that you really hope all his dreams of wealth and happiness comes true.

His love interest, Jasmine, also offers up more than standard Disney princess material. Implored by her Sultan father to accept a suitor, Jasmine finds herself frustrated and bitter with the old ways of her culture. She wants to choose her own husband on her own terms and does not appreciate being seen as a prize. In a moment where Aladdin and Jafar bicker over who is best suited for the princess, Jasmine proclaims that she doesn't love either of them and storms off. Aladdin will have to work for her hand rather than cover it in riches as he initially hoped would do the trick.

Similar to Disney's other animated films of that era, *Aladdin* went through many changes before settling on its style and story. Initially pitched in 1988 as more of a campy musical by Howard Ashman and Alan Menken, the original script featured the genie appearing more as a Cab Calloway type and Aladdin appearing with his mother and a trio of friends. The project was initially shelved for disinterest, but was back in preproduction with Ron Clements and John Musker taking over. Though Ashman and Menken did compose a few musical numbers in their draft, the majority of their work was omitted from the picture by request of the producers.

The songs of *Aladdin* were not as catchy as *The Little Mermaid* or *Beauty and the Beast* in that they were faster with higher energy (mostly from Williams' eccentric numbers). But if you can keep up with the quick pace of the lyrics, they are fun to sing along with. "A Whole New World" is the most memorable with its slow and romantic tone, but "Prince Ali" and "You Ain't Never Had A Friend Like Me" take a bit of practice to keep up with Williams' singing. But as time goes by, you'll find that these songs are at least memorable enough to sing loudly in a bar with your best friends. Or at least for me they were.

The film did come under fire by American-Arab Anti-Discrimination Committee for the song "Arabian Nights". In the theatrical cut, the song featured the lyrics "Where they cut off your nose if you don't like your face". For the video release, the lyrics were rewritten and rerecorded to "Where it's flat and immense and the heat is intense". Since the edit wasn't made until the video release, the first soundtrack release featured the original lyrics, only to be revised in future releases.

As with any Disney picture, there is the myth of secret lewd content inserted into the picture. During a scene where Aladdin is playing with the tiger Rajah, a quiet bit of improvised and muffled dialogue seems to sound as if Aladdin is saying "Good teenagers, take off your clothes". According to the directors, the dialogue improvised was actually "Good tiger, take off and go". Even with the explanation, Disney still decided to remove the line from the DVD release to put the controversy to bed.

And there was yet another controversy with similarities to Richard Williams' *The Thief and the Cobbler* (1995). Though *Cobbler* was released in different versions over the course of the 1990's, it had actually been in production for decades. Similarities can be seen in the story, scenes and characters. In particular, the character of Zigzag appears as a combination of Genie's blue features and magical powers as well as Jafar's wicked beard and mustache. Due to the edits made to make the film more of a musical, *The Thief and the Cobbler* was seen more as an *Aladdin* copycat film even though it came first.

The proof that only Robin Williams could inhabit the character of Genie was made very clear by the direct-to-video sequel *Return of Jafar* (1994). Genie's voice was replaced by Dan Castellaneta, best known to many as the iconic voice of Homer Simpson. He would additionally voice the character of the Genie in the *Aladdin* animated TV series. While Dan does an admirable job for stepping into such lofty shoes, it just wasn't the same. Thankfully, Williams did return to the role for the third film in the series, *Aladdin and the King of Thieves* (1996).

The reason Williams' did not return for *Return of Jafar* was the result of a falling-out he had with Disney. His pay for the picture was only $75,000 on the condition that Disney would not make his character predominant in the marketing or advertising of the film. Williams wanted this so it wouldn't detract from his other film, *Toys* (1992), which would be released one month after *Aladdin*. Disney failed to comply with Williams' wishes and it caused him to leave Disney. It wasn't until the new management at the studio issued a public apology did Robin Williams decide to return to the role for one more animated feature.

Aladdin has plenty of firsts as a claim to fame in both visuals and performances, but it still manages to pack just as many thrills and hilarity as it did in the theater. The mystical elements and cultural decadence carry an exhilarating sense of adventure. The humor, despite Williams' mass usage of pop culture references, has a timeless quality that all ages can enjoy even if the parodies of Jack Nicholson and Peter Lorre go right over the heads of the little ones. If they're familiar with other classic Disney pictures, they'll at least be able to spot the cameos by Pinocchio or Sebastian the crab from *The Little Mermaid*.

BAMBI

I watched a great deal of Disney animations as a child with the advent of Disney Classics VHS releases, but *Bambi* (1942) spoke the most volumes. It was dazzling for its bold and vibrant view of a woodland forest containing eye-catching animal creatures. It was engaging in how the dialogue never droned on with needless exposition or uninteresting elements. Of course, most kids will recall the film as being a more traumatic experience for the haunting death of Bambi's mother.

I could recall the scene quite vividly in my youth, replaying it over and over in my mind. The mother and her fawn tread lightly through the meadow when Bambi's mother can hear the distant sounds of man. In a flash, she shouts for Bambi to run as fast he can to the woods and not to look back. The music grows tenser as Bambi moves his small little hooves at maximum speed. The music stops when a gunshot is heard from behind. It's all over now - Bambi's mom is killed off-screen. Bambi does not realize this until he has already made it back to the thicket alone.

The tragic realization sets in that his mother is not coming back. Bambi wanders through the deserted forest, shouting and crying out for his mom that will never return. The chorus swells and the snow begins to fall. Just as Bambi is about to breakdown in his wailing, the Great Prince deer frightens him into silence with his looming presence. The tall and powerful figure gives Bambi a straight look and states what needs to be said: "Your mother can't be with you anymore." Before receiving safe passage back home, Bambi looks back where his mother may have once been with one tear escaping his eye. It is the end of childhood.

The whole scene sounds rather extreme for a Disney animated film, but that's what makes *Bambi* such a notable classic. It's a coming-of-age story that showcases the beauty and pain of growing up.

Film critic Roger Ebert explained it best in a cameo on the drama *Early Edition*. A child appears depressed outside a movie theater after witnessing a *Bambi* knock-off film about bunnies. Ebert is called upon to explain to the child why the story had to be written with the mom's death. He explained that if the mother bunny didn't die, the little bunny would never have gone off on his own to have an independent adventure. Such a talk leads to this wonderful exchange:

"Does my mom need to die?"
"Of course not."
"Why?"
"Because you're not a rabbit."

But *Bambi* is not just about the tearful gloom of mortality. The forest itself is teaming with the wonders of life, perfectly punctuated by the music. As raindrops slowly descend on the plants and trees, the orchestra matches the pace of the rain while the chorus begins to chime in with drips and drops. The chorus also doubles as the voice of the wind and thunder. Bambi looks on with amazement and fear at the falling water as the various animals scurry for cover and warmth.

As the newest member of the woodland community, the film takes joy in Bambi's discoveries. He struggles to stand up on his thin little hooves as the friendly rabbit Thumper steadies him. Loud and talkative, Thumper imparts his wisdom of greens and language. He takes it upon himself to help with Bambi's speech, trying to get him to properly pronounce the word bird. When Bambi finally spits it out correctly, he is overjoyed that he trots around repeating one of his first words. He quickly makes friends with the cuddly skunk Flower, spending his days lounging in brightly colored plants. He plays with Thumper on an iced-over lake where the small rabbit attempts to help his pal stand and slide on the slippery surface.

Even after the demise of Bambi's mother, the film still finds joy in the fascination of a teenage buck discovering romance during mating season. Playfully retitled as the season of "twitterpating", it is a time when Thumper and Flower soon find themselves attracted to the opposite sex of their own kind. Bambi soon discovers that there is more to his childhood friend Faline than he first thought. But he'll first have to prove himself by locking horns with another jealous deer for Faline's hoof in love.

There is tremendous craftsmanship in *Bambi*'s world with so many little details in the design. The Disney studio had previously animated some animals for *Snow White and the Seven Dwarfs*, but Walt wanted a higher level of realism in movement this time around. The woodland creatures would take center stage and they needed to be convincing as central characters. *Snow White*'s creatures were too busy crowding scenes with movement that was all over the place. It was forgivable since they appeared more as set decoration, but they could not be as strangely fluid if they were to be the focus of the story.

For reference, the animators not only drew inspiration from the Los Angeles Zoo, but also from a zoo Walt Disney had setup at the studio. The small enclosure was filled with woodland creatures including two fawns which were named after the central couple in the film (Bambi and Faline). The animators constantly studied their subjects with plenty of reference drawings and sketches to give them a feel for how to make these characters believable. They had to find the right mixture of realism and personality. This meant not only having animal references, but human references as well. Skaters Donna Atwood and Jane Reynolds helped to provide a display of falls for the animators to be used in the scene where Bambi attempts to walk on ice.

Another Disney first was that the characters in *Bambi* would age over time, requiring both multiple designs and voices. In particular, there were about four voice actors for the role of Bambi at various stages in the film. Despite a rather large assortment of actors to play a handful of characters, the film is very sparse on dialogue. Walt Disney found the original script too talky and made major changes, carving it down to less than 1,000 words.

Great care was taken not just with the characters, but the environments as well. The backgrounds of the woodland area truly come alive with lavish designs layered many times over with the multiplane camera. The studio had previously used the multiplane camera with their other animated features, but it was used with such grace in *Bambi* the way it took the audience deep into its world. Artist Maurice Day truly encapsulated this microcosm having snapped many reference photos and sketched many drawings in the forests of Vermont and Maine. Combined with the impressionist painting style of animator Tyrus Wong (later appointed as art director on the project), the resulting backgrounds were beautifully rendered yet simple enough to not be too distracting from the characters.

While it's easy to look back on certain Disney productions as major cash cows for merchandising, many of the early productions after *Snow White and the Seven Dwarfs* were not that successful. *Bambi* not only suffered a loss at the box office, in part of World War II restricting the European market access, but also received negative criticism upon its release. Audiences were more used to Disney's trademark of magic and fantasy, but *Bambi* appeared far too grounded in reality. There was actually mass disapproval from many American hunters over the film's portrayal of humans slaughtering animals.

There is certainly an implication that man is a destructive force in the picture, but also a faceless one. We never see a full-figured shot of the slayer of Bambi's mother or the hunter who assaults the forest in the second act. There was a figure to be seen in a looming shadow, but that drawing only made it as far as a storyboard that was not used in the film. The distance between the animals and man keeps the film focused, avoiding any hammered in commentary about nature and environmentalism.

It doesn't matter who is shooting at the animals as there is no wider recognition of the circle of life. Somebody is shooting at them and they are running for their lives. Although I suspect that the hunter of the second act was drunk on his outing given how he seems to be randomly firing at every creature in the area from birds to chipmunks. Either that or he was incredibly desperate for food. I can't imagine small chipmunks have much meat.

As with *Pinocchio*, Disney's *Bambi* diverged from the darker aspects of the original novel. Most of these changes were for the sake of not making the picture too violent as the source material was considerably bloodier. But it is rather surprising how much of the violence remains in the film and how effective it is at dealing with death. A deer is shot, two deer battle to the death and a panicked bird is shot out of the sky. There was even going to be a sequence where the hunter meets his end by his own stupidity, but it was eventually cut after negative testing.

Over the years, *Bambi* was released several times over in theaters for many decades until its acclaim grew to the level of Disney classic. Despite several negative reviews and a disappointing box office, it eventually reached its rightful praise having garnered a 91% rating from the Rotten Tomatoes website. It is now more than worthy of the classic title bestowed on its many video releases.

When one of my college buddies made an outing to the Disney store, she asked our group of friends what their favorite Disney movie was. I, of course, answered with *Bambi* since I had acquired the latest Anniversary Edition on DVD and couldn't get enough of it. She returned the next day with a present for each of us - a plush from our favorite Disney picture. I received a small, soft Bambi doll with its legs locked in a bent sitting position. Throughout college, it became a conversation piece I perched on my desk which led to many talks about one of my favorite Disney animated films. It looks cute on the outside, but holds so much more on the inside.

BAREFOOT GEN

Perhaps the most horrific vision of the atomic bombs obliterating Japan would have to be the nightmarish artistry of *Barefoot Gen* (1983). We do not witness the explosion from a distance, but are placed right at the epicenter. A child screams out in terror as her flesh is charred and her eyes melt from their sockets. A mother uses her remaining seconds of life to cradle her burnt baby. A dog barks at the bright flash and tries to escape, but is melted against a fence from the heat.

Glass shatters and buildings collapse with people inside them. The young schoolboy Gen looks up at the explosion. The student next to him has half her face melted by the exposure which Gen avoided by being behind a wall. When Gen comes to after being blown back, he witnesses large groups of radiation-engulfed people walking among the wreckage as if they were the undead.

These are the disturbing images that *Barefoot Gen* places in our mind and it does not shy away from the grotesque aftermath for a moment. The film never wastes a chance to showcase a pillow shot of a dead body or a land destroyed. When Gen goes out looking for food in the wake of the explosion, he spots soldiers loading up charred and radiated corpses onto a truck with no care taken into handling them. Holding his nose while witnessing members of his own neighborhood now as mere husks, Gen remarks that this must be what hell is like.

But the bomb doesn't drop at beginning of the film as the first half builds up the characters of Hiroshima. We see Gen as a typical Japanese schoolboy, filled with energy and determination to be a man. He and his brother Shinji take on various day to day tasks to keep their family safe and healthy. They work in the wheat fields with their family and make an attempt to acquire a carp for their pregnant mother. Lessons about family and courage are brought about with a

16

coming-of-age structure.

There is a threat with B-52 bombers assaulting Japanese cities, but it doesn't seem as serious to Gen and his family living in Hiroshima. They've already had some false alarms with air raid sirens and the more immediate threat is the shortage of supplies. Gen's mother Kimie is facing an ill pregnancy without the proper medicine she needs. Gen's father has been open about his distaste of the Japanese military which has bred distrust from their neighbors.

Thirty minutes into the movie, we eventually reach the morning of August 6th and the big bomb finally drops on them. Though Gen's family survives the initial blast, Gen and his mother can only watch in horror as their entire family burn to death while crushed under their home. Gen's father offers his final words to his surviving son that he must now be a man to help protect his pregnant mother. As their family burns, Kimie begins laughing hysterically in a temporary state of insanity. The surrounding citizens in the area are now charred and melting beings wandering aimlessly around the destruction. It is entirely on Gen at this point to grow up quickly and watch over his ailing mother.

Eventually led to a safer area by a neighbor, Kimie soon has the baby prematurely. With no midwife or supplies, Gen must help deliver the baby on his own. He is successful in aiding his mother to give birth to a baby girl. Gen later decides to help the wounded survivors by offering them water, but the contamination only speeds up their demise. The boy witnesses both life and death within a few hours.

The last act focuses on Gen trying to be brave amid all the deaths that follow in the aftermath of the bomb. Even after the wounds have been healed and the cadavers disposed of, the radiation remains that sneaks up on several individuals. Hair comes out in clumps and bowels bleed as more continue to die. Though trying to remain strong, Gen also faces the harsh nature of reality. He is infuriated when he hears the Japanese only surrendered after a second bomb was dropped. He is terrified when he discovers his hair is falling out, fearing that he has radiation sickness. He becomes so frustrated with the lack of food and abundance of death that he cries out to the spirit of his father for guidance. Gen must not only find the strength to be a man, but the hope to continue on.

Barefoot Gen was based on a comic book series by Keiji Nakazawa who tries to relay much of his first-hand experience with surviving the explosion. The film retains his drawing style in featuring characters with big eyes, oversized mouths and rounded features. The characters appear more innocent than serious as if the picture was going to be a more sweet drama of a Japanese family during a time of war. It's a trait that adds to the shock value when the bomb finally drops on Hiroshima.

When I first saw *Barefoot Gen*, I was horrified and shaken by the experience. I found it almost inappropriate the way such graphic displays of the aftermath was animated in the stylized anime design. I blocked most of the imagery out of my mind to focus on other animated films. Whenever somebody brought up the film in conversation, it would always be referred to as the messed up film with the atomic bomb explosion. Most everyone into Japanese animation is familiar with the key scene of the explosion for the graphically detailed vaporization of Japanese civilians as a gross-out money shot.

Coming back to the film was not easy at all. As a parent, I was twice as slugged in the gut by the shocking images of children being destroyed and abandoned. As the burnt people walk aimlessly through the aftermath, a crying child blindly tugs on her mother's dress. A mother lying against a tree topples over as her baby cries and hopelessly tries to suckle any remaining milk from her breasts. I was on the verge of not even including this film in the book simply for how emotionally draining it was to watch on a second viewing as much as it was the first.

But the whole point of the film is to be disgusted and for good reason. War is not glamorous or PG-13. It destroys human beings in ways that we cannot even fathom. I took note how even at the end of the film - after all the shocking and tragic death that befalls many characters - Gen still finds some hope. He is incredibly ecstatic upon discovering a sliver of grass growing in the ground when everyone else said nothing would grow there for many years.

It seems odd to imagine how a child could remain so chipper and determined after witnessing one of the worst atrocities in human history. But children seem to react differently to the worst elements of life. Gen doesn't wallow in tears at the grave misfortune for his family and his city. His back remains firm with tears in his eyes, but faith in his heart. This development of character, clutching to the remnants of childhood, prevents the film from being just a guilt-trip or a depressingly shocking expose on atomic bombing.

Barefoot Gen is unsettling, off-putting and surreal. It is not an easy film to watch and it is certainly one that haunts the viewer long after the credits. But it's a picture that deserves to be seen for those very reasons as a chilling reminder that while Americans saw a bright cloud of victory, the Japanese witnessed a new level of inhumanity.

BATMAN: THE MASK OF THE PHANTASM

Out of all the interpretations of Batman on the big screen, *The Mask of the Phantasm* (1993) is the one entry that is largely forgotten, but fondly looked back on once remembered. It wasn't just a case of being lost to time. Even when it was first released into theaters Christmas of 1993, nobody seemed to be talking about the picture until a few months later when it hit video stores. Even Siskel & Ebert did not get around to reviewing it on their movie review program until almost a year later and actually felt silly for overlooking such a stylish animated film (especially when it shined brighter next to the grim *Batman Returns* and lukewarm *Batman Forever*).

The truth is that the theatrical release of *Phantasm* was a bit of an afterthought since this was originally intended to be a direct-to-video movie. The decision to go theatrical was dropped on the filmmakers while the film was already in production with mere months to meet the theatrical release date. Despite being rushed, the studio did grant them more control over the project and a bigger budget to make the animation shine for the big screen. Director Eric Radomski had to move fast and redesign shots to fit a theatrical aspect ratio. The result was one of Batman's lowest grossing theatrical films, but one of the best incarnations by far.

While director Tim Burton was struggling to make a more outlandish and action-packed Batman for theaters, executive producer Bruce Timm and his animation team were working on an entirely different level with *Batman: The Animated Series*. Timm's crew loved the Batman comics and knew how to make his universe work in animated form for kids and adults alike. They knew how to create a Gotham that was dark and noir, but not garish and grizzly. They knew how to use every Batman character without going too campy or too practical. You bought into the superhero format and never once felt like the show was talking down to its audience with such stories.

This became very clear to me in 5th grade. My class convinced the teacher to turn on the television in the afternoon. It was my teacher's first time seeing *Batman: The Animated Series* and it was the episode where Batman was locked in an asylum while infected with Scarecrow's fear toxin. Batman has a terrifying vision of his parents disappearing down a dark tunnel which rises from the ground to form a giant gun, dripping either sewage or blood. Our teacher sat in shock for something this dark being in a kid's cartoon.

"You kids watch this stuff?" he asked.

We all nodded in excitement with our stupid grins. And every afternoon since, he'd be gunning to turn on the television more than the class, hoping to catch more of the show. I knew then that *Batman: The Animated Series* was more than just another cartoon intended for kids.

The Mask of the Phantasm is a testament to the animated series that redefined superheroes in animation. It beefs up the budget for the big screen not to be bigger and brighter than the TV series, but provide a slicker canvas for an engaging mystery. The opening sequence is the most decadent of the film featuring a computer-rendered version of Gotham that we gracefully fly through as the opening credits roll. Notice how it doesn't feel out of place for the color or design of the city that appears in the rest of the film.

Batman's villain for the picture is a masked killer referred to as the Phantasm, an original character appearing as if the Ghost of Christmas Future were a supervillain with a hook for a hand. He is targeting a string of gangsters and staging their deaths with Batman's name written all over the crime scenes. Now wanted by the cops more than usual, Bruce Wayne will have to keep his cowl low on his path to clear the name of Batman.

What makes the film work isn't so much the mystery itself, but rather the dressing around the crime. Bruce Wayne's past plays a heavy role as he finds himself dwelling on his early adult years as an orphan. He recalls a time before the costume when he was just starting out as a masked vigilante in Gotham. Bruce believes he has his life of crime fighting all figured out until the right woman walks into his life.

In one of the most emotional moments of the film, Wayne visits the grave of his parents to air his bitter frustrations at finding a woman who loves him. "I didn't count on being happy" are the tearful words he mutters while begging forgiveness for not continuing his reign of vigilante revenge on crime. His parents most likely smiled down on him to find such love, but Bruce is so conflicted by his crusade that he believes he must be a grim avenger. He's frightened by the fact that he may not be doing enough in his acts of vengeance. It's that vulnerable side of Bruce Wayne we rarely see portrayed in the other Batman films and never with such emotional realization.

Prior to this tearful exchange with himself, he meets this perfect woman in the same graveyard. Andrea talks to her dead mother as well, but with a more carefree attitude as if she's not taking it too seriously. It doesn't take long for the two to hit it off especially when they finally share a kiss after displaying their fondness for jujitsu. They also share each other's pain when Andrea confronts Bruce talking to his parents' graves by embracing him in the pouring rain.

There is genuine romance and emotion between Bruce and Andrea that develops in their younger years. Time passes, Bruce devotes the rest of his life to becoming Batman and the councilman Reeves aggressively makes a move for Andrea when she returns to Gotham. As Andrea slowly reconnects with Bruce when she returns to Gotham, we learn that the two of them have grown bitter and depressed from the forces that tore them apart. Drink in hand, Andrea insults Bruce's quest to avenge his parents. He leaves while she throws the glass on the ground in tears. They've both been transformed by tragedy and they fear it will never get better. A series of flashbacks progressively reveal how their love led to tragic heartbreak.

The mystery of trying to solve the true identity of the Phantasm gives Batman much more to do than punch out thugs or dole out his Bat gadgets (though there is a stellar sequence with the Bat-jet). Bruce actually does his homework in tracking down the trail of mobsters that leads to the masked killer. The surprise reveal of the Phantasm isn't all that shocking, but it is rather clever how the picture gets to this point. I did admire how the picture stuck to its guns with trying to portray a real mystery and romance for the caped crusader rather than just hand him a familiar villain with a familiar scheme. The Joker doesn't even show up until about halfway through the picture and is mostly a supporting antagonist.

The animation style matches the bold contrasting colors of the TV series. Angular designed characters with plenty of shadows are portrayed against a dark Gotham City. The backgrounds were so heavy with black that the designers actually painted on black paper to save time and color. The soundtrack is brilliantly operatic with conduction by Shirley Walker, co-composer on Tim Burton's *Batman* (1989) and the regular composer for *Batman: The Animated Series*. Most notable about her score is the addition of a choir that can be heard over the opening theme and several of the more dramatic moments in the picture.

The film didn't exactly feature any big voice talents. Kevin Conroy and Mark Hamill reprise their roles as Batman and Joker from the TV series. Dana Delany, who voiced Andrea, was a regular voice on the show and would later become the voice of Lois Lane on *Superman: The Animated Series*. The guest starring voices are mostly relegated to secondary roles. Abe Vigoda and Dick Miller perfectly fit the bill as aged mobsters and Stacy Keach brings his deep voice for the Phantasm as well as other characters.

This is a case where the cast is more about nailing the voice than adding marquee value. Voice director Andrea Romano has a perfect ear for bringing these DC Comics animations to life. While working on *Batman: The Animated Series*, notable actors were cast such as Ed Asner, Paul Williams, Henry Silva, John Vernon and Dave Warner. They're all very common in the realm of cartoon voices, but none were that notable to the pop culture landscape of the 1990's. But when you listen to their voices, you can feel them giving genuine performances. Romano did not want to cast actors that would try to do cartoon characters – she wanted actors that would exude their natural voice to achieve a true performance. In particular, Kevin Conroy and Mark Hamill have become iconic as Batman and Joker that they've reprised the roles numerous times for other DC Comics animated series, direct-to-video movies and video games.

While *Mask of the Phantasm* never garnered enough of a box office to warrant more theatrical animated features for the caped crusader, its success on home video launched a wave of direct-to-video DC Comics movies that continue to be produced as of this writing. Following *Mask of the Phantasm* were three more direct-to-video Batman movies: *Sub-Zero* (1998), *Return of the Joker* (2000) and *Mystery of the Batwoman* (2003).

Soon after Bruce Timm and his team finished work on the animated series *Justice League Unlimited* (2004-2006), they focused all their efforts into more direct-to-video features with more adult stories ripped from the comics. It was the perfect platform where directors and writers could target the DC Comics stories they wanted to animate with a PG-13 rating. Most notable of these is the 2-part *The Dark Knight Returns* (2012-2013) which perfectly captures Frank Miller's version of an aged Batman in a grizzly Gotham.

For an animated movie based on a TV and comic book series, *Mask of the Phantasm* ascends past its limited constraints of budget and demographics. Diverging heavily from the dark and strange nature of Tim Burton's *Batman*, Bruce Timm and company crafted a Batman movie about mysterious murders, mafia gangsters, lost love and pathos. IGN ranked it as one of the best animated movies of all time, Time Magazine called it one of the 10 best superhero movies ever and Wired Magazine dubbed Kevin Conroy's performance as the best Batman of all time. Even as Batman's theatrical presence matured with the coming of Christopher Nolan's trilogy, *Mask of the Phantasm* still holds up with a plot that doesn't involve a villain trying to destroy Gotham City. That seems to be a rather lofty goal for villains who are constantly foiled by a man in tights.

BEAUTY AND THE BEAST

Prior to the Disney Renaissance of the 1990's, animated films were not as well regarded at the Academy Awards. Despite massive achievements in the medium during the 20th century, it was not until 2001 that the Academy finally added the Best Animated Feature category. Perhaps there was finally enough competition in the medium of animation to warrant its own award. Others speculate that they just didn't want animation creeping into live-action categories as the quality of animated features was reaching higher levels that could compete with the best of live-action films.

After *The Little Mermaid* (1989) had already made Disney's presence known for winning awards in the area of music, *Beauty and the Beast* (1991) achieved another milestone by becoming the first animated film to be nominated for Best Picture. If the addition of the Best Animated Feature category was an attempt to keep animation in the corner, it failed when *Up* (2009) became the second animated feature to be nominated for Best Picture. *Toy Story 3* (2010) followed it up by being the third nominated. You just can't stop Disney.

The success of the Disney Renaissance can best be attributed to digging up old ideas and giving them a musical twist. Much like *The Little Mermaid*, *Beauty and the Beast* was based on pre-production ideas that began in the golden era of Disney. Dropped and abandoned due to issues with conceiving the story, it was revived from the boost of energy and interest during the production of *Who Framed Roger Rabbit* (1988).

The feature was originally going to be a traditional narrative structure that made its way pretty far through production, but was eventually scrapped when the success of *The Little Mermaid* provided a more profitable template of musicals. This was a good call considering that three of the songs from the picture were nominated for an Academy Award, guaranteeing a win. *Beauty and the Beast* was also the first Disney animated feature to be turned into a Broadway musical which garnered a Tony award.

When I initially watched the Blu-ray release of the film with my wife, she heard there was some new footage added and thought it applied to the "This Prudential Life" opening sequence. I assured her that this sequence was unaltered from the original theatrical release and she was amazed at how vivid it appeared in high definition. Partial credit is due to the restoration team who did a fantastic job with the transfer, but the works of the animators truly stand the test of time for the brilliant use of movement, color and shading.

Belle's morning stroll through town is brimming with life at every corner. A child chases a pig in the background, only to be chased by the pig one second later. A distracted barber snips off half a mustache. A mother with babies crawling all over her pleads for eggs. Accompanied by a memorable and catchy tune, it's an energized way to introduce the audience to both the book-obsessed Belle and the pompous hunter Gaston's intentions of marrying her.

When Belle is captured by the frightening Beast, a selfish prince cursed to a furry form as he secludes himself in his old castle, she slowly begins to warm up to him. She attempts to understand him by bringing him into the light. She soon discovers that he's just as frightened as she is upon their first meeting. Their romance begins to bloom and there is a race to see it develop. If it doesn't, the curse that has befallen Beast and his servants will prevent them from ever being human again.

What makes *Beauty and the Beast* stand out as Disney's finest of animated features ultimately comes down to the characters in both design and personality. For the character of the Beast, animator Glen Keane drew inspiration from numerous animals including buffalo, bears, wolves and gorillas. The result is a character that can appear fearsomely savage in the darkness, but tenderly frightened in the light. He shares a shyness and fear in dealing with Belle as she may be the one that can lift the curse. He's protective and vicious, only later displaying his gentler side when he realizes blunt force won't win him the heart of the girl.

The brute stud Gaston was conceived by animator Andreas Deja as a muscular jerk, inspired by the vain men that would trot around Los Angeles. He's a character that is handsome and knows it to the point where he believes he has the entire town under his thumb. This makes him the perfect villain for the picture as one filled with egotism and narcissism. Gaston also has one of the most amusing musical numbers, aptly named "Gaston", where he shows off his masculine and chauvinistic nature to the tavern patrons. He starts fights, marvels at his array of mounted animal heads and even boasts of his burly chest hair.

Even the characters of the servants, cursed to the bodies of common castle items, have a surprising amount of unique qualities. Lumière, a maître d' transformed into a candlestick holder, uses his romantic nature to push the Beast towards Belle as kindly as he can. His constant need to break the rules in the name of love grinds the gears of the stubborn Cogsworth, a strict butler transformed into a clock. There's the motherly presence of the teapot Mrs. Potts and her teacup child Chip. The role of Chip was originally a short one (as in one line), but later expanded with how impressed the filmmakers were by the voice performance of Bradley Michael Pierce. His cute dialogue is much appreciated; most notably after he's transformed back into a human and asks his mother if he still has to sleep in the cupboard.

The most iconic scene of the picture, paraded in nearly every television ad, was the ballroom dance sequence. It was a pivotal scene in establishing the exact moment when Belle and the Beast were comfortable with each other. It was enchanting with Angela Lansbury providing the softly sweet vocals of the theme.

But what impressed audiences more than anything was the use of computer graphics to generate the ballroom. With every inch of the interior computer generated, the camera was able to flow smoothly down from the chandelier, over the heads of the couple and dolly beneath them with a low shot. The characters themselves are hand-drawn and were composited into the computer generated environment. The effect creates a stunning sense of depth and focus that can still be felt to this day. Whereas most computer graphics from this era show their age, this sequence remains timeless in its mastery of design and staging.

The breathtaking animation was ultimately a result of Pixar's CAPS (Computer Assisted Production System) which provided a digital ink-and-paint system first used on Disney's *Rescuers Down Under* (1990). The system created a stunning level of soft shading and a large of array colors on top of the traditional hand-drawn animation. Belle's skin appears with warm shadows as she strolls through the field in the evening and her face has the slightest blush when she admires the Beast in a snowy setting. It was most likely this use of CAPS that earned the system a Scientific and Engineering award from the Academy of Motion Picture Arts and Sciences in 1992.

A unique aspect which benefited the story was the addition of screenwriter Linda Woolverton. Most animated films are developed more through storyboards than a script as was the case with Disney's previous animated features. Linda wrote the original draft first and then began working with storyboarding teams to develop it into animation. Her talents continued on as a Disney screenwriter as she wrote the script for *The Lion King* (1994) and would later pen Disney's live-action productions of *Alice in Wonderland* (2010) and *Maleficent* (2014).

The musical numbers are first-rate and by far Disney's finest work in the area of memorable numbers. Howard Ashman and Alan Menken wrote the initial music, though Ashman was a little reluctant as he was concentrating more on *Aladdin* (1992) at the time. Over the course of production, many of these songs would be retooled. "Be Our Guest" changed from Lumière singing to Belle's father into Lumière singing to Belle. The title song was to be a rock ballad, but was revised to be more touchingly romantic after Ashman and Menken coaxed Angela Lansbury into singing it.

The only song that was omitted from the theatrical release was "Human Again" which featured the transformed servants singing about how wonderful it will be when the curse is lifted. The song would later be revised for the 1994 Broadway stage production was later animated into the Special Edition re-release of the film from 2002. The animation for that sequence, created with the same CAPS method and updated technology, is not too shabby for trying to match the style over a decade after the film's release.

The songs were written by Ashman and Menken at a hotel in Fishkill, NY as Ashman was dying from AIDS. He passed away a mere eight months before the film was released. At the end of the film's credits, a tribute is placed in his honor reading *"To our friend, Howard, who gave a mermaid her voice, and a beast his soul. We will forever be grateful. Howard Ashman: 1950-1991."*

The acclaim of *Beauty and the Beast* has led to it being one of the most cherished of Disney classics. Upon its initial video release, it was one of Disney's first animated pictures to have a video release of its workprint which was previously screened at the 1991 New York Film Festival. It was selected in 2002 by the Library of Congress to be preserved in the National Film Registry. It has been re-released theatrically for both IMAX (2001) and Disney Digital 3D (2010). But no matter how many different video formats or theatrical presentations it receives, *Beauty and the Beast* remains a timeless animation treasure that is inviting to guests of all ages.

THE CASTLE OF CAGLIOSTRO

The Japanese comic book character Lupin the Third (semi-based on the French thief character Arsène Lupin created by author Maurice Leblanc) could be considered a cartoon James Bond sans the class. A creation of the artist Monkey Punch, Lupin was an international thief would hop around the globe swiping riches with his partners in crime.

His comic book series, a cross between an action serial and a Playboy illustration, has made him one of the most iconic and adult stars of Japanese comic books and animation. Throughout the 1970's, there were some stellar animated adaptations that brought all of Lupin's crass, sexiness and debauchery to the big and small screen. Lupin's first feature film, *The Mystery of Mamo* (1978), retained the gleeful tone of the comics with its trippy subject matter and saucy adult content. The protagonist is portrayed as such a horny devil that he's mastered the technique of literally jumping out of his clothes to get in bed with a woman.

But Lupin's second feature film, *The Castle of Cagliostro* (1980), is one of the most divergent portrayals of the character. Lupin appears in this picture as a gentler version of the thief, less of a womanizer and more of a clever goof. He seeks more adventure than pilfering and fawns over the damsel in distress more tenderly than any woman he's ever interacted with before.

To tamper with such formula almost seems blasphemous as the character has retained these larcenous features in most of the movies, TV series and TV specials. Who would reimagine such an iconic character of perversion and crime? It was a rising director at the time known as Hayao Miyazaki, years before he established the much renowned Studio Ghibli.

Miyazaki was no stranger to Lupin, however, given his work on the first Lupin TV series from 1971. He co-directed the second half of that animated series with Isao Takahata, another great animation director in the rough who would also direct some Studio Ghibli productions. Both of them desired to make Lupin more of an upbeat and plucky character as opposed to the devilish playboy he appeared as in the early episodes of the TV series.

That playful aspect of Lupin stuck with the character, appearing far more as a giddy joker in the second Lupin TV series from 1978 (of which Miyazaki guest directed two episodes). From Miyazaki's early work on the Lupin series, you can see his influence and future ideas all over those episodes. He wants to inject a sense of adventure and wonder as well as making the female characters more powerful and unique as opposed to sexual eye-candy.

As the first feature-length animated film directed by Hayao Miyazaki, *The Castle of Cagliostro* contains all of his spirit and ideas for the Lupin universe, even more so since he wrote the script as well. In the first scene, Lupin and his accomplice Jigan have just busted out of an international casino, dashing to their yellow Fiat with overstuffed bags of money. They hop in their car with the money - completely covering their faces in cash - and drive off as the gun-toting security goons scrambles to their vehicles. Rather than proceed with a high-speed chase, Lupin had enough foresight to disable their vehicles with tires falling off and frames falling apart. An apology letter is left on the inside of one of the car hoods.

The two laugh at their new fortune, but change their tone when they realize the money is counterfeit. Rather than get angry in violent frustration, as Lupin tended to do quite often in his past incarnations, the thief grins at the prospect of tracking down the counterfeiters. They open the sunroof of the car and start throwing the money out of the moving vehicle with glee.

I'd be ecstatic as well if my next stop was a glorious European countryside. The credits roll over their road trip through the beautiful landscapes, passing by trains and young women walking alongside the road. They stop briefly for the night to share a meal over a small campfire and relax with a cigarette before heading back on the trail. All these backgrounds have a bold and colorful appeal, especially when set against the whimsical opening melody of vocals and light orchestra. In various English versions, this opening was chopped and replaced with still images to cover up the Japanese credits. Those editors should be ashamed of themselves for omitting one of the best opening credit sequences to any animated feature.

Lupin and Jigen's destination is the tiny country of Cagliostro, rumored for its counterfeiting operations which many snoops have never returned from investigating. On their way into the central town, they encounter a car chase where some thugs are gunning after an escaping bride. Choosing not to resist some excitement, Lupin takes off for the girl in his speedy Fiat, defying gravity and physics with its ludicrous maneuvers. To catch up with the bad guys, he drives sideways up the roadside hill that hugs the road, accelerates through a forest at the top of the hill and back down the hill sideways once again.

After defeating the bad guys, but losing the girl, Lupin is left with her wedding ring as a clue that unearths a secret part of his past. He's been to Cagliostro and seen that bride before as the shy Clarice, a little girl who saved his life after a failed heist. Lupin's quest is still focused on the treasure, but it's also become a mission to rescue the beautiful Clarice from being forced to marry the evil Count of Cagliostro. With his finely combed hair and devilishly thin mustache, the Count is a classic antagonist who desires Clarice more for the riches she is worth than her beautiful heart.

It just so happens that both the illegal counterfeit operation and the marriage transpire at the legendary Cagliostro Castle, a decadent palace of aqueducts and traps. Several characters sneak around the castle via the classics: passing through bookcases opened by the push of a book and spying behind walls through the eye holes of paintings. The Count keeps his future wife locked away in a separate tower that is only accessible from a retractable skyway bridge. The onsite security consists of stern royal guards and automatic laser-firing robots. This castle would be the envy of every James Bond villain.

As Lupin prepares for his great break into the castle, he assembles all the necessary players for any of his capers. Goemon, the stoic swordsman, quietly makes his entrance onto the scene. He remains silent for the majority of the picture, only opening his mouth or unsheathing his sword when he feels the situation warrants it. Lupin's eccentrically aggravated nemesis - INTERPOL agent Zenigata - pops up at the castle as extra security. He's spent his entire life hounding Lupin with over-the-top determination and is fully expecting the great thief to strike again. Lastly, Lupin's love/hate nemesis Fujiko is already in the castle and working undercover for her thieving goals.

What is most intriguing about *Cagliostro* is the genesis of how Miyazaki's future films materialize in this picture. We see his obsession with old and unique aircraft the way the Count favors an Autogyro, displaying shades of *Porco Rosso*. We see elements of the strong female hero from *Nausicaä* in the form of the innocent Clarice and the feisty Fujiko. He transforms the gruffer Jigen and Goemon into much more dashing and gentle giants, reflective of how he treats most of his male side characters in future films.

Ever present is Miyazaki's love of large and open landscapes as there are several quiet moments to take in all the beauty. While Jigen changes the tire of their car, Lupin sits on top of the sunroof smoking his cigarette and enjoying the silence of the peaceful green hills. Lupin later takes an evening stroll through the ancient ruins of Cagliostro - slowing down and taking a reflective sit. These are exceptional moments of a deep breath before all the manic caper fun starts up again.

If there was an iconic scene that stands out from *Cagliostro* it would be the chase through the innards of an active clock tower. Dashing away from gun-toting guards, Lupin and Clarice make their way up through the tower and its many large gears and spokes. They dash through the spinning parts of the clock with the evil Count leaping towards them with his sword.

It's hard to deny the inspiration for a similar scene in Disney's *The Great Mouse Detective* (1986). While that film was more notable for its computer-aided animation of the clock tower, *Cagliostro* is rather special for featuring such an intricate sequence in hand-drawn animation. Lupin uses the sheer force of the whirring machinery to build up enough momentum to smack off the villain's helmet with a wrench. Miyazaki frames this scene as a wide shot where we can see both the positions of the Count and Lupin as they duke it out on constantly moving platforms.

What's more intriguing about Miyazaki's version of Lupin is that *Cagliostro* seems to suggest a more mature version of the character that has grown since his childish days. When Lupin flashes back to the early years of his thieving career, we see a manic individual driving through walls, swiping diamonds from a jewelry store and gambling with hot women surrounding his aroused expression. These quick shots give the impression that this is a life he has left behind.

While it's always been amusing to follow Lupin as the playboy thief, Miyazaki finds a new dimension to the character by allowing him to grow and reflect without depleting any of his charm. He snickers like a cat when faced with impossible odds, but takes the threats more seriously when a woman's life is on the line.

No other incarnation of the characters has he ever been more of a gentleman thief. Lupin swoops into Clarice's cage of a darkened bedroom to deliver a poetic and romantic rant that he caps with a tiny flower festooned with tiny flags. There's something about his expression in that scene which suggests he may have used this line to charm a girl or two before, but here he's using it more sweetly to add a dash of hope for escaping the Count's clutches.

Even as Miyazaki's earliest feature predating Studio Ghibli, the film was a tremendous influence on the industry. Pixar co-founder John Lasseter admits to being inspired in his career from viewing a clip of *Cagliostro*. Gary Trousdale, co-director of *Atlantis: The Lost Empire* (2001), was inspired by the ending of *Cagliostro* and ended his picture with a similar scene of the receding waters of a sunken city. There was even a rumor that Steven Spielberg was impressed by the picture as well, but there's little evidence to support this despite a quote from him appearing on one of the DVD releases.

The film continues to charm to this day as it is recognized as one of Miyazaki's best. Though the Lupin franchise never carried on much of the heroically noble traits and tones into future incarnations, it remains one of the strongest of the Lupin movies and built the foundation for the genius of Miyazaki. If he could bring wit and charm to a character that was a thief and a pervert, he could please just about anyone with his animation direction.

CLEOPATRA, QUEEN OF SEX

From such an erotically suggestive title, one might assume that *Cleopatra, Queen of Sex* (1970) was a pornographic movie. It's certainly what Americans thought when they saw the nudity on the poster and the X rating in 1972. But when erotic moviegoers attended the theatrical screenings and discovered a lack of graphic sex scenes, they promptly demanded their money back. Why the X rating? It was actually self-imposed by Xanadu Productions in hopes that it would play to the perverted crowd based on the modicum amount of nudity and sex present in the animation. It may have also been to stand out as the first X-rated animated film for American theaters, but that title went to *Fritz the Cat* which was released the same year with a more deserving and official X rating.

Its original title in Japan was simply *Cleopatra* and the film was intended more as a comically surreal take on the life of the iconic woman. The director of this project was Osamu Tezuka, best known as the godfather of Japanese animation for creating the first Japanese animated TV series *Astro Boy*. Tezuka is an artist that approaches animation with his own style and brand of humor. Take a look at his lengthy comic book adaptation on the life of Buddha where he sticks to the central events, but doesn't shy away from inserting visual gags whenever he can. His style can run the table of tones, jumping from violent battles to silly moments of slapstick. Nothing is out of bounds to him in the realms of comics and animation. If it looks entertaining, he goes for it.

Cleopatra begins with one of the oddest fusions of animation and live-action I've ever seen in a film. Taking place in the future, live-action footage of characters was shot with their faces drawn over with animated character designs. It's a strange choice and the effect appears rather stilted the way the animators seem more concerned with covering the human faces than drawing them with more life. But the odd nature of such a sequence does help set the tone for this script that wants to play around with the historic material less as historians and more as Chuck Jones.

The story is oddly told and seen through the eyes of men and women from the future that transfer their souls into bodies of the past. Their mission is to learn all they can about Cleopatra and what her name means for a certain secret attack plan by galactic forces. Once we've gotten most of the sci-fi angle out of the way, the story moves to ancient Egypt for the more historical aspect of Cleopatra through Tezuka's wild vision.

When displaying scenes of war, a cartoonish approach is taken to make scenes of death and turmoil seems more crazy and creative. A soldier slices the heads off a peasant and his goat - their severed heads fly up in the air and land on the opposite bodies. It may seem strange to be making light of such violence, but Tezuka isn't exactly approaching this material with historical sensitivity.

When Tezuka does approach historical events, he puts his own cartoonish spin on them. The historically cited first meeting of Cleopatra meeting Caesar when she was rolled up in a rug and snuck into the palace by Apollodorus is present in the picture. But in the setup to that scene, Apollodorus contorts Cleopatra into a ball, pushes her into the shape of an egg, shoves her into a sack and tightly straps it shut. When she is unfolded nude in front of Caesar, his reaction goes from comical shock to sexual intrigue. Another comical take on historic events is how Caesar's famous murder by his betrayers is played out in the form of a Japanese play.

The gags of *Cleopatra* seem to sneak up on the audience without expectation. When Cleopatra calls out for help in one scene, the film quickly cuts to Tezuka's robot Astro Boy character flying through the sky with his heroic theme as a one-shot joke (a trademark of Tezuka was including cameos of his other characters). In that same scene, two gladiators battle each other with a giant flyswatter and a pistol. The comedy is not bound by the era in even the slightest.

The humor can best be equated to that of *The Naked Gun* or *Hot Shots* where all the characters play it straight. In the scene where Cleopatra attempts to murder Caesar in Rome, she does so under cover of night with a pistol in her hand. When discovering more of Caesar's strange mannerisms that affect her true feelings for him, she continues to hold the pistol in hand. There are several moments such as this that give the viewer the option of either following along with the plot or laughing at the historically inaccurate elements intentionally inserted.

The animation never bores in this picture as it is constantly changing in style. During a city celebration, the imagery shifts to a more painterly quality as random works of art appear in the crowd. A nude Mona Lisa gives a wink to the camera. The Birth of Venus clam is wheeled across the road. The Burning Giraffe figures introduce a burning giraffe into the parade, as well as a burning rhino and a burning pig. This entire sequence is so absurdly out of place that I can't help but admire the film's tenacity with throwing anything it wants at the screen. Tezuka also takes advantage of using wild colors. Caesar is colored with green skin, explosions can be seen with more pink than orange and blood splatters at the screen in hues of green against backgrounds of black.

Though the film has its moments of war, drama and romance, it is most consistently a comedy - one of the most surreal comedies that could be conceived for such material. There are moments of violent brutality as when a slave throws a spear that pierces through the neck of a horse and into the torso of the riding soldier. But then there are more baffling moments during a naval action scene with several quick cuts. The cuts range from boats burning to men on toilets to drowning men to drunken octopuses. The whole sequence is so fast and frenetic with imagery that bounces from silly humor to war drama. Tezuka never settles for one tone.

The addition to the American title of *Queen of Sex* isn't entirely unwarranted. There is quite a bit of nudity and sex, both sensual and comical. A slow-motion sequence in a bath features Cleopatra being ravaged by Caesar. The camera slowly pans over different curves of her body partially submerged in waters of pink and purple. In another scene where Cleopatra has sex with Mark Antony, the film seems to jitter and cut off of the frame as if the projection had a malfunction. I can only imagine how much this scene angered those American audiences who came to see hardcore animated sex only to be met with such a ridiculous tease.

Cleopatra, Queen of Sex is perhaps the most obscure of the entries in this book because it was a rather big failure in both Japan and America. The picture was a major loss for Mushi Productions which led to Osamu Tezuka leaving the company to form his own production studio. Mushi Productions was so desperate to stay afloat that they sold the American rights to Xanadu Productions in 1972 for a pornographic release. The reviews for the American release were horrendous, mostly based on the false advertising that angered several audiences expecting something more sexual than comical. Tezuka, angered at his work being promoted as pornography, was pleased to see its American release fail.

The film was perhaps too avant-garde and esoterically strange for its own good, in addition to being poorly marketed. But there is just something about its weird and surreal nature that makes it a uniquely clever and hilarious picture. Where it fails as erotic cinema, it pleases as an undisciplined and rebelliously silly piece of adult animation.

COONSKIN

Throughout the history of animation, there has been much political incorrectness on the subject of race. Several cartoons from the *Looney Tunes* golden age featured blackface and stereotypes of African-Americans that were omitted for television broadcasts (though preserved on the DVD sets for historical purposes). Disney's *Song of the South*, despite winning an award for its catchy tunes, has since been buried by the studio as much as possible to forget such a misstep in southern perceptions of blacks. Chances are you'll never see that animated film legally on home video from Disney.

But *Coonskin* (1975) doesn't want to cover up these caricatures or polish them for politically correct approval. It wants to be offensive and exaggerated with an uncomfortable atmosphere, forcing the audience to process such harsh satire in its portrayal of race. This was Bakshi's perspective of growing up on the streets of Brooklyn, coated with his signature adult animation style where nothing was off limits. Being the boss of his own studio and movie, Bakshi made *Coonskin* as he saw fit, drawing from past experiences and readings on black culture. This control led to several rewrites based on Bakshi's conflicting and evolving opinions.

As a satire of *Song of the South*, the movie begins with live-action footage of two black men, Randy and Pappy, escaping a southern prison. While they wait for their ride, Pappy regales Randy with a story told in animation. This is no simple tale of Brer Rabbit, but rather an urban story of Brother Rabbit, Brother Bear and Preacher Fox. The anthropomorphized characters ditch the sunny south and head for Harlem which they foolishly believe will be a welcomed haven for black people. They are dismayed to discover that Harlem is a bitter land of gangs and corruption.

From this point, the movie becomes a smattering of heavy and controversial satire. Many of it will leave the audience questioning its uncomfortable and avant-garde nature. Sometimes it's blatant: A black minstrel attempts to woo a female embodiment of America, only to be lynched when the woman smugly cries rape. Other times it's artistically subtle: A gangster's wife transforms into a youthful figure which shrinks into a winged creature upon being murdered.

The importance of just about every one of these strange scenes is that it leaves us constantly questioning what it means and what we should feel. How exactly would you interpret the sight of Aunt Jemima hunting down a waffle with a pistol? Is it a commentary on racism, stereotypes, commercialism or greed? Is it all of these or none of them? I still find myself coming away with a different theory and feeling each time.

Bakshi creates an uneasy distance of race throughout the picture. A rich white couple invites a group of black people to their party. The couple chats with them about how wonderful and progressive they believe themselves to be for inviting such colorful characters into their home, treating them as rare and remarkable anomalies in their world. The white couple appears as live-action actors, prim and proper. The black people appear as cartoon characters, exaggerated with big lips and pitch-black dark features. Both are cartoonish stereotypes.

The most chilling aspect is how Bakshi goes directly into political cartoon mode with some of the characters. America itself appears personified as a tall, big-breasted blonde in tight star-spangled clothing. A mafia member appears as a gay prostitute in cowboy attire and a John Wayne accent. A black minstrel dances on the streets in large clothing with stereotypical mannerisms. These are all caricatures that are blunt, uncomfortable and loaded with messages both simple and complex.

While Bakshi peppers the picture with plenty of difficult symbolism, there are a few scenes that stand out as uncomfortably forward in their message about race. A white man is covered in blackface to give the appearance of a black man. Angered after being harassed, he runs into the street in his underwear, wildly waving a gun. A horde of police arrive on the scene and order him to put his weapon down. Before the blackfaced white man can process this information, he is shot down by the police.

The shooting is not quick nor is it subtle. Bullet after bullet pierces the man's body with blood gushing from nearly every wound.

The message couldn't be any clearer. There is a racial hypocrisy that breeds violent confrontations with the law that certain people can't comprehend until it happens to them. Most of this sequence is in slow motion to showcase not just the brutality, but give the audience a moment to ponder what might be going through this man's brain before it hits the pavement.

As of this writing, the jazz soundtrack for *Coonskin*, written and performed by Chico Hamilton, has never been released. A noteworthy track is the opening number "Coonskin No More" that was performed by Scatman Crothers (the lyrics were by Ralph Bakshi). Described by Bakshi as an early form of rap, the song has the uncomfortable nature of a plantation melody with blunt lyrics about racism.

Race is always a touchy topic and a film so blunt and brutal with its focus on African-Americans was not met well initially. Even before the film had debuted, there was controversy. Bakshi had finished the movie on a Friday, screened it in California on a Monday and then screened it in New York at the Museum of Modern Art on a Wednesday. That Wednesday, before the screening, there were already picketers protesting the film outside the building. Bakshi found it interesting how hysterical people reacted at the screening to a movie they hadn't seen yet. When Bakshi asked present racial activist Al Sharpton why he didn't want to see the film before it was screened, Sharpton simply remarked, "I don't need to see shit; I can smell shit!"

The Congress of Racial Equality deemed the film offensive and racist while the NAACP supported it as a difficult, but necessary, satire of racism. The film did gain a cult following and was eventually held up as one of Bakshi's strongest films. But when first released theatrically, *Coonskin* went through waves of protests at theaters for showcasing the film and at Paramount for distributing it. Paramount handed over distribution rights to the Bryanston Distributing Company.

As a result of its Blaxploitation release, the Bryanston Distributing Company releasing the picture went bankrupt only two weeks after the film debuted. There were even some cases where smoke bombs were thrown into a theater by protesters to force audiences from seeing the picture. While filming *Taxi Driver* in Times Square, Martin Scorsese sent Bakshi footage he shot of audience members fleeing a theater from such an incident.

Despite being a commercial failure with a circus of controversy, Bakshi considers the film a masterpiece. And he's not alone considering the film has been admired by the likes of Spike Lee, Quentin Tarantino, Richard Pryor and the Wu-Tang Clan. In particular, the Wu-Tang Clan expressed interest in producing a sequel.

On the introduction to one of the *Looney Tunes* DVD collections, Whoopi Goldberg explains how some of the cartoons on the set are racially offensive. While she admits that they are as wrong now as they were then, she recognizes that these shorts are a part of history, offensive though they may be. Those shorts have been preserved for a restored presentation as a reminder of that era and the racial problems of such times.

Bakshi, too, doesn't want us to forget. He doesn't sweep such vulgar interpretations under the rug. He's not seeking to open old wounds, but wants to rip off the social gauze to display how time has not healed all. No element is softened or spoon-fed. When *Coonskin* wants to show violence, it's brutal and bloody. When *Coonskin* wants to display racism, it showcases the worst of bigotry. When *Coonskin* focuses on the hardships of the ghetto, it doesn't tone down the sadness or disgust. And when it wants to be funny, it's never an easy laugh.

FANTASIA/FANTASIA 2000

Walt Disney's most ambitious project was his anthology animated feature *Fantasia* (1940). He had already succeeded in elevating the animation medium out of exaggerated shorts and into big feature films with *Snow White and the Seven Dwarfs*. But *Fantasia* was going to be so much more than just another animated feature for his studio. He wanted to take the medium and expand it from just being a movie to an experience akin to the opera.

The man was no stranger to working with music given his work on the animated shorts of *Silly Symphonies*. He found a mutual friend in this department with composer Leopold Stokowski who was so willing to lend his orchestral talents to animation that he would work for nothing. With Stokowski's collaboration, Disney set out in 1937 to create one of his most lavish and memorable Mickey Mouse shorts, "The Sorcerer's Apprentice".

But when the costs for the production grew far too high, he knew he'd have to turn it into a feature. He could keep "The Sorcerer's Apprentice", but also add in more animated shorts using just as powerful music. This little project, which Walt conspired with Stokowski on, was initially dubbed "The Concert Feature".

This would be one of Walt's most experimental animated features in which a tidal wave of ideas flooded onto the screen. Though "The Sorcerer's Apprentice" doesn't begin or end the picture, it is the most iconic and memorable of the segments. It certainly stands out as the most cohesive and faithful story following Mickey Mouse as the one central character - a sweeping assistant and admirer of a powerful magician. The magician goes to sleep, Mickey swipes the hat, brings his broom to life and chaos ensues. The sorcerer of this sequence was modelled after Walt Disney which can be seen in the face with the raised eyebrow. The sorcerer was even given the name of Yen Sid (spell it backwards).

The film opens with one of the most abstract of segments, "Toccata and Fugue in D Minor". It begins with live-action footage of the orchestra and then transitions into a mix of shapes, lines and patterns. German artist Oskar Fischinger, known for his abstract animations, was called upon for this sequence initially. Ultimately, though, Walt rejected Fischinger's bombarding vision and kept "Toccata and Fugue in D Minor" slightly more grounded. Lines would form violin bows and clouds could be seen in the background, creating a sense of orientation with all the flowing geometry.

"The Nutcracker Suite" does away with the dancing toys and is replaced with a blooming forest of wonder. Fairies gracefully dance along flowers and little mushrooms perform a Chinese dance. There's still the sense of a ballet, but through the natural forms of leafs and fish. The amazing techniques for this sequence, combining airbrush and drybrush, took about three to four hours to produce each frame according to animator Ward Kimball.

"The Rite of Spring" transports the viewer to a savage age of dinosaurs that fight for survival as Earth violently shutters with volcanic changes. It's a journey that takes us from the wondrous stars of creation to the apocalyptic end of the dinosaurs. The research needed for creating "The Rite of Spring" had the animators studying everything from comets to baby alligators. Various experiments with bubbling liquid, smoke and even paint entering water was used as reference for creating a volcanic environment of boiling lava and billowing clouds. The dinosaurs themselves appear large and with weight the way they slowly stomp around the screen with low camera angles. So massive was this sequence it was actually planned out to be longer with the evolution of humans, but was shortened to avoid controversy from creationists.

"The Pastoral Symphony" was a fanciful portrayal of Greco-Roman mythology in which a festival for Bacchus is interrupted by Zeus' lightning bolts. The festival is filled centaurs, cupids and fauns. The most unique additions were the female centaurs. Centaurs were a very different figure for the Disney animators to work with, but the female centaurs were especially challenging in deciding how much you should show of their bodies. Animator Ward Kimball had a large stack of memos on how these characters should be drawn in a variety of shots that he found rather humorous.

"Dance of the Hours" brings a satirically comical approach to this piece of ballet music. Disney animators walked a fine line of realism and comedy for this sequence. They studied ballet with plenty of reference and then applied the performance techniques to alligators, elephants, ostriches and hippos. The attention to movement, weight, staging and lighting easily make this one of the best pieces of character animation in the film in addition to being the most funny.

"Night on Bald Mountain" is a sequence about evil with the Slavonic god Tchernobog awakening from a mountain to summon spirits from their graves. The spirits dance around in his large palm until they are squashed with a laugh. With Tchernobog's demonic powers, gargantuan size and sinister form against the darkness of night, it is perhaps one of the most frightening displays of pure evil. What's most scary about this portion of the film is that Tchernobog is never really defeated. He simply recoils back into the mountain as daylight approaches and the Witches' Sabbath ends.

When *Fantasia* was released on VHS, one of the television promos featured an eager dad watching the film with his smiling infant son. Curiously missing is the moment when they reach "Night on Bald Mountain", the infant cries and dad stays up all night trying to comfort the child from the resulting nightmares. At least the segment is quickly followed up by the more peaceful "Ave Maria".

The musical segments are presented with connecting live-action bookends of an orchestra against a colorful background. Leopold Stokowski is seen conducting the Philadelphia Orchestra with Deems Taylor acting as presenter of each section. Only once do we see Mickey Mouse appear during these sequences and it's only briefly to have a small chat with Stokowski. It creates a real sense of an event rather than just another stellar animated feature from Walt and company. It also feels real in how one introduction is momentarily paused when something goes wrong with one of the instruments in the orchestra.

Fantasia spent three full years in production and had its share of discoveries and problems. The final sequence of "Ave Maria" faced technical problems that had to be fixed just one day before the premiere. In attempting to create the illusion of a live orchestra in a movie theater, collaboration with Disney and RCA resulted in the creation of stereophonic sound. At the time, the process was dubbed as Fantasound. Being the most ambitious of Disney's early features,

Fantasia was not a box office success. The cost was $2,280,000 to produce, $400,000 of which was spent on the music. It wasn't until the third release in 1956 that the picture broke even.

I'm including both *Fantasia* and *Fantasia 2000* (1999) in this entry per Walt's intention with the project. He wanted *Fantasia* to act as a sort of touring concert that would return to theaters ever so often with new additions as well as old favorites. Though it was never updated under Walt's rule, there were plenty of plans for new shorts that included a fantastical view for "Flight of the Valkyries" and a quiet vision of "Clair de Lune." These segments were never finished, but some made it pretty far in production as seen on the special features of home video releases. "Flight of the Valkyries" made it as far as storyboards and "Clair de Lune" actually has some finished animation.

It would not be until the year 1999 that *Fantasia* would grace the big screen once again with additions. Though it was mostly comprised of new animated shorts, as well as celebrity introductions to each piece, it still featured "The Sorcerer's Apprentice." The short was not remade or digitally altered for a widescreen presentation; it was presented just as it was seen back in 1940 with the color and sound partially remastered. It's the only returning short, most likely only included for Mickey's iconography, but it's still very welcome.

Fantasia 2000 (1999) became an amazing pet project of Walt's nephew Roy Edward Disney. The new segments retain the original format of the first film. James Levine conducts the Chicago Symphony Orchestra on a stage that also makes room for the animators to perform as well. Various celebrities were chosen to host the interstitial segments including James Earl Jones, Angela Lansbury and Steve Martin. Their sequences are amusing and rather fitting as when Penn and Teller introduce "The Sorcerer's Apprentice".

The opening animation is an abstract vision of Beethoven's 5th Symphony where simple colors of light and dark masquerade about the screen like a flight of butterflies and bats. Though it's the most abstract of all the shorts, it's much more character driven than that of the lucid "Toccata and Fugue in D Minor".

"Pines of Rome" depicts humpback whales flying around icy oceans and into a supernova. As the first sequence suggested and animated for *Fantasia 2000*, started as early as 1993, the story evolved from the penguins' perspective of whales to the tale of a lost baby whale. Computer animation aided in the natural grace and girth of whales while traditional hand-drawn animation provided the emotion of their eyes. The result is a segment that stands out with grand beauty and wonder with its deep blues and greens.

Al Hirschfeld's curvy style of character design is lovingly applied in a busy city vision set to "Rhapsody in Blue". The animation was all hand-drawn and then colored in the computer, resulting in highly expressive characters with a naturally cool color palette. Various characters seeking a different life find themselves caught up in the hustle and bustle of city life. A construction worker dreams of playing drums. An unemployed man finds himself struggling to acquire a job. A chipper little girl longs to spend more time with her parents. All of the storylines converge in an amusingly frenetic climax. The segment contains many nuggets of homage as with the insertion of the letters "NINA" into the ridges of a toothpaste container - a tribute to Hirschfeld's daughter.

"Piano Concerto No. 2" features a tin soldier trying to woo a ballerina. It was one of the few segments that carried on from Walt's early concepts in the 1930's. The backgrounds were competed by hand while the characters were entirely CGI. Pixar was at one time considered for animating this sequence, but director Eric Goldberg had convinced supervising director Hendel Butoy to let the Disney animators handle it on their own. Pixar probably didn't want to repeat what they had previously done either by animating more toys after having worked on *Toy Story* (1995) and *Toy Story 2* (1999).

Considering the incredible technique of ballet and form from "Dance of the Hours", *Fantasia* animator Joe Grant wanted to bring some more of that graceful character animation to *Fantasia 2000*. For "The Carnival of Animals", an eccentric flamingo amuses himself with a yo-yo while disapproving flamingos aim to take it from him. The flamingos were originally ostriches, but they were changed to avoid Disney repeating themselves. Directed by Eric Goldberg, the sequence is vibrantly colorful with its watercolor paintings and computer graphics. Goldberg appears drawing at a desk in the introduction for this sequence as James Earl Jones introduces.

Donald Duck finally gets a shot at *Fantasia* for his place in the "Pomp and Circumstance" piece, portraying the religious story of Noah. It's a simple bit of romantic drama as Donald and Daisy hurry to usher all the animals aboard the ark before the big flood. The two of them are separated from each other in the shuffle. They both end up on the ark, but neither of them sees each other aboard and believe their love is lost to the flood. Of course, they miss each other at every turn on the ark and are not reunited until they finally reach land. A simple and somewhat cliché plot, but still perfectly staged with plenty of dialogue-free humor. Donald checks off a couple of anatomically correct ducks to board the ark, perplexed at the confusion in evolution.

Aiming for an ending that matched the duality of good and evil from the first film, "Firebird Suite" is the most emotional and magical pieces of the picture. A sprite awakens from the cold of winter bring about Spring with her powers of nature. She changes forms as she begins to create flowers from her hands and coats mountains with a wave growing grass. A volcano spirit halts her progress and burns down the forest to ash, but she soon rises forth to bring back life with the help of a friendly elk. This particular piece was a beautiful marriage of both 2D and 3D animation - the elk's body is traditionally drawn while his antlers were CGI.

Both *Fantasia* and *Fantasia 2000* represent a more experimental form of animated features. They're bound by ideas that spring forth more from the minds of the animators than pens of writers. Story supervisor Joe Grant noted that all they had for a story were musical notes, trying to find the right images that fit with the music. What an exciting experience to let loose with your ideas and dreams to match such a beautiful score. Ralph Bakshi once said that if you listen to music and you're not daydreaming, you're not listening to good music. Walt Disney was clearly listening to good music, perhaps more closely than any other filmmaker of his generation.

FANTASTIC PLANET

When you mention the medium of cutout animation, the first example that might pop into your head would be Terry Gilliam's animated segments for *Monty Python's Flying Circus*. Gilliam would cut out pictures and current photographs of various icons and figures to create robotically moving characters with frame-by-frame animation. Tiny, moveable pieces of paper had to be carefully moved for each frame for the desired effect. Click the camera, move slightly, click the camera, and move slightly. It seems like such a painstaking process that I have to wonder just how crazy Matt Stone and Trey Parker were for using this technique initially on *South Park* (they later streamlined the process through computer animation software).

But Rene Laloux's *Fantastic Planet* (1973) - based on Stefan Wul's 1957 novel - lifts that animation format out of the comical and into something surreally trippy. It's the type of sci-fi spectacle which seemed only possible in books that I couldn't imagine it being as successfully translated to the screen outside of animation. It's a wondrous film to be sure, but it still is a powerful story in how it dabbles in speciesism, superstition and hints of the Cold War era.

Human beings are referred to in the film as Oms (a corruption of the French word "hommes" which translates to men), appearing as the size of mice when next to the giant alien society that looks down on them as pests and pets. The aliens are referred to as Draggs - blue creatures with bulbous eyes and webbed ears appearing as nightmarish visions of sea monkeys. The Draggs live much longer than the Oms and thus do not reproduce as much. They're aware of the tiny humans, but only in the sense of them being rats. They're a menace in droves, but individually can be treated as pets.

A group of Dragg children corner a female Om with her baby, pushing and pulling at the small woman. After accidentally killing the mother during play, the Dragg child Tiva happens upon the baby and decides to take care of the orphaned infant Om as a pet. She calls the little Om boy Terr and raises him from a baby to a teenager, keeping him in line with a magnetic collar and forcing him to do tricks.

The education systems for the young Draggs comes in the form of a headset device that beams information into their minds. Terr is able to leach off some of this info by being held by Tiva during her lessons. As time progresses, Terr becomes more intelligent and eventually decides to run away with Tiva's learning device. He scampers off into the harsh alien badlands to seek the company of the secret society of Oms. They are not as accepting of him at first as there are those who do not trust a domesticated Om. He will have to gain the trust of the many tribes to band together and find a new planet they can call home.

The world of the Draggs is a fantastically surreal dream of beautiful terror. The Oms journey through a land packed with all sorts of bizarre creatures. A giant bird with a tree trunk for a beak protrudes its sticky tongue into a log to pull out occupying Oms for his lunch. A pink blob entrapped in an organic cage uses the tentacles of his nose to pluck flying creatures from the sky and smash them into the ground for amusement. Creature after creature fills the screen as if plucked straight from your strangest nightmares.

The Draggs themselves are rather odd aliens that are capable of out-of-body meditations in addition to manipulation of their bodies. A foursome of Draggs sit in a room of contemplation where their eyes go white with thought as their bodies blur, stretch, twist and contort into all sorts of weird shapes. Tiva curls up into her bed like a snake as her legs disappear into a coiling tail.

It's all weird and strange, but there's logic to everything on screen. Tiva takes Terr outside to witness a ground infestation of crystals that seem to grow quite quickly. Terr gets his leg stuck on one of them and the crystals soon begin to consume him. With a mere whistle, Tiva is able to shatter the crystals and release her pet. Terr tries whistling as well to become acquainted with his surroundings, shattering more of these growing crystals.

The human tribe of the Oms has their own customs for deciding on every aspect of their living. To settle feuds of power, two combatants have sharp-toothed creatures attached to their chests which do battle to the death. In the carnal act of procreation, the men and women cover themselves in a bright glow as they chase each other into the darkness of night for passionate sex. Their ultimate goal is to escape to the moon where they discover nothing less than the unexpected.

The picture carries with it plenty of themes, but rarely batters the audience with such topics as racism and xenophobia. The only time they seem to be truly blunt occurs during a scene where the Draggs hunt down the small humans. A small device whirls across the ground and shoots out pucks that emit poisonous gas. The Draggs proceed through the gas with tiny humans on leases to sniff out their own. The presence of gas masks on both the Draggs and the humans carries an eerie tone of the cold war. The various deaths of the Oms, from magnetic spike plows to deadly spotlights, would disorient the viewer to the fragility of human life on a world we do not control. Sometimes it's comically dark and other times it's shockingly grotesque. Perhaps there is something more to say in this picture about how we view violence in an untamed world where words and ethics are seemingly useless.

The animation is very limited in movement with a mix of hand-drawn and cut-out animation, but is absolutely gorgeous in its design. The characters and backgrounds resemble the highly detailed artwork of European artists from issues of the comic magazine "Heavy Metal". By keeping the drawings and movements to a minimum, the animators are able to move artwork with a great deal of gradation and different forms of shading. Most of this style was the work of writer/painter Roland Topor who drew most of the designs and cutouts, but left the project before the animation process began.

Most notable about the cutout aspect is that there is no armature to the way characters move. Whenever an arm or leg moves on a character, it is hand-drawn animation. Whenever a simple shape is moved across the screen - such as a large hand reaching into a shot - it's pushed through with cutout animation. The favoring of both techniques creates believable characters that can move believably with immense detail.

Since there wasn't much of an animation industry in France at the time, Laloux employed Czech animators and used a Czech studio that was normally used for puppetry. Production began in 1968 before the Soviets invaded the country. Coincidentally, *Fantastic Planet* has an eerie similarity in its story to the enslavement of the Czech people.

Armed with its trippy imagery and progressively psychedelic rock score, *Fantastic Planet* is often seen as a drug trip movie. The Draggs seem to indulge in bizarre methods of mediation and take literal head trips towards the end of the picture. Upon first viewing, some may remark that the filmmakers must have been on drugs to conceive such a strange animated film. Despite the look and tone of counter-culture, the inspirations for *Fantastic Planet* came from different places. The original novel was typical science fiction of the 1950's. Roland Topor was inspired by surreal art. Rene Laloux's odd nature came from his earlier days of working at a psychiatric institution where he made his first film. The only person who seemed to be about the LSD culture was Roger Corman who produced the English version for American theaters.

Rene Laloux directed two more animated science fiction films after *Fantastic Planet*. *Time Master*s (1982) was based on another novel by Stefal Wul ("The Orphan of Perdide") and the screenplay was co-written by famous artist Jean Giraud (aka Mœbius). *Gandahar* (1988), better known as *Light Years* in America, was animated in North Korea and had an English translation revised by famed author Isaac Asimov.

Fantastic Planet has much to showcase with its challenging parables and surreal artistry. There's savageness and beauty to this fully realized world of great wonder and weird horror. A consistent tone of the real and unreal can be felt throughout, echoing odd sensations only felt in the most perplexing of dreams. It's sure to please potheads that want something to trip out to, but also give the squarer of us a real film worth watching and dissecting.

FINDING NEMO

Pixar's early works managed to tap into the finer interests of childhood that lead to another world. Kids and adults could relate to the emotions placed in toys and the curiosity placed in monsters being in your closets. With *Finding Nemo* (2003), they delve into a world that appears wondrous to all ages. What kid didn't marvel at the fish tank in the doctor's office or get lost in the amazement of the aquarium? It was the allure that director Andrew Stanton had with the aquatic world that led to Pixar's fifth animated film.

The story has a genuine appeal for both kids and adults, allowing both the parent and child of the picture to proceed on an adventure. The nervous clownfish Marlin, perfectly voiced by a panicky Albert Brooks, becomes frightened and determined to find his son Nemo after he is kidnapped by a scuba diver. As Marlin finds himself exploring the many miles of sea that separates him from his child, Nemo attempts to get back to his father through a jailbreak situation in a fish tank.

Parents can relate to the plight of Marlin as an overprotective father. Stanton based this aspect on how concerned he was for his son's safety during a walk in the park. It's a great arc with a lesson for the older audience members to loosen up or you'll miss all the best moments of raising a child. The younger audience will be able to identify with the plucky Nemo and his banding together with a group of sea creatures to escape back to the ocean.

We still have to deal with the death of one parent as Nemo's mother perishes before his birth, but in her place is the more eccentric female fish Dory. With her short-term memory and overly energized attitude, she was a character perfectly suited for the voice of Ellen DeGeneres. Ellen was chosen for the role based on how quickly she could change conversations over a short period of time on her talk show. Dory was such a likable character in her ignorance and innocence that she would eventually receive her own movie, *Finding Dory*. Her charismatic energy is always present in the way she finds a game in any obstacle and believes she can speak the language of whales.

The world of *Finding Nemo* is rather remarkable in how there exists different societies and mannerisms of animals above and below the ocean. Marlin and Dory happen upon a group of sharks that have formed a support group dedicated to curbing their appetite for fish ("Fish are friends, not food"). Sea turtles approach their traveling with a California surfer vibe. Packs of seagulls fight over food where the only word they know is "mine". This creative construction of character makes every step of the journey more engaging with the anticipation of what unique creatures our protagonists will meet next. There are also plenty of surprises in the way that Marlin and Dory hitch a ride in the mouth of pelican rather than end up as its dinner. The characters were so charismatic that Pixar broke their streak of bloopers in the credits to give each character a final bow of sorts.

Despite being confined to a dentist's fish tank for the majority of the picture, Nemo's escape ends up being just as tense and exciting as Marlin and Dory's odyssey. The tank-occupying characters that include starfish and blowfish have a surprising amount of personality in how they conspire for their grand exit. They also embody their own culture as Nemo is sworn into their society with his own special name. The initiation scene was an inspiration that came during a six-hour car drive to Los Angeles where director Andrew Stanton and screenwriter Bob Peterson would discuss the story as they drove.

With each Pixar film, there is one aspect of the animation that amazes and attracts the audience. People couldn't stop talking about the amazing fur effects of Sully in *Monsters Inc.* or Violet's long hair in *The Incredibles*. The grand visual draw of *Finding Nemo* is its underwater environment. Everything from the swaying of reefs to the caustics of the underwater lighting is beautiful and alluring. The attention to detail owes much to Pixar's dedication to research. Executive producer John Lasseter insisted that every person on production go scuba diving to experience the world that they would be creating.

The technical team behind creating the underwater setting was given live-action footage as a test to see how close they could match it with computer animation. The tests came back with astonishingly realistic results. In fact, they were too realistic in that you couldn't tell the CGI from the live-action footage. Pixar then pulled back and tried to find the right level of design that was both believable and had a unique style. The end result is a detailed water environment built for different levels of day, depth and surrounding aquatic life. The waters can appear murky, sunny and in deep blue. There's sewage water and small aquarium water that all feels accurate and intoxicating to the eyes. The underwater sequences were so pleasing that Disney gave the audience more of that ambience by including a virtual aquarium special feature on the *Finding Nemo* DVD. This may partially explain why the film was one of the best-selling DVDs ever produced.

The aquatic characters were given just as much attention as the environments. In addition to giving them all a wide range of emotion for their facial features, much care was taken into the research of the various creatures. Many a dead tropical fish easily found in pet stores were slapped on scanners and intricately observed by the art department for texture and lighting. Quite similar to the process of the environments, the animators took reference footage of fish and matched the swimming movements with the computer-generated characters. Naturally, some liberties had to be taken to deliver the type of story Pixar was aiming towards. Adam Summers, a professor of physiology that provided lectures and input to the animators, argued over certain points in the animation that fins don't work the way the animators made them work. An animator responded, "Adam, fish don't talk."

Finding Nemo became so popular that the obsession eventually led to controversy. Despite the manner in which the film seems against the capture of clownfish, the depiction ultimately led to a surge in the order of clownfish as pets. On the other side of the coin, however, others were inspired to set their pet fish free in the ocean which ended up disrupting aquatic ecosystems. If there is any applicable message to the picture, it would be not to mess with the wonders of the deep, good intentions or otherwise.

Environmental concerns aside, *Finding Nemo* has that special touch of an all-encompassing Pixar masterpiece. It's cute enough for kids, smart enough for adults and spectacularly vivid for all ages. In many ways it resembles Disney's classic efforts for *Bambi* where enough research and effort was put into the picture that the audience cares about a fish escaping from an aquarium or fleeing a horde of seagulls. The film won me over so effortlessly that by the end I didn't even mind the easy choice of Frank Sinatra's "Somewhere Beyond the Sea" for the ending credits. And even if I did, I could just hit the mute button and still enjoy the visual splendor of the CGI ocean.

FRITZ THE CAT

Fritz the Cat (1972) is legendarily referred to as the first adult animated feature for its X rating. For the home video release, it was marked down to an R rating. Decades after its release, I've heard several people argue that the film is not even worthy of an R rating, implying that it could be PG-13. I'd like to believe they haven't seen it in years since I don't exactly see how a film with loads of drugs, heaps of nudity, very bloody violence and some fairly graphic sex scenes would garner a PG-13. But the MPAA seems fairly crooked in their ranking so maybe I'm wrong. One thing that can be said for sure is that *Fritz* was unlike any other animated feature in that you never saw Bugs Bunny smoke a round of joints or Mickey Mouse sexually congregate with Minnie Mouse (at least not in any of the cartoons that I've seen).

At the helm of this groundbreaker was director Ralph Bakshi, an animator previously known for Saturday morning cartoons of the 1960's. Though quickly rising up in that market, Bakshi aspired to greater ideas. He took a look at the current state of the world with its heated protests and war in the streets that it just didn't feel right animating such simple distractions. He wanted animation to be more personal and truthful with an air of honesty not present in the sugary landscape he dabbled within.

The first animated feature he wanted to create with such a quality was *Heavy Traffic*, but his producer Steve Krantz initially shot the film down since executives would be less likely to fund a first-time animation feature director (especially for an adult animated film which wouldn't thrill them either). But when Bakshi picked up a copy of Robert Crumb's underground comic book *Fritz the Cat*, he knew he had to collaborate with such a talented and vocal mind. Crumb was already swimming in the bohemian soup of counter-culture art and Bakshi wanted to do for animation what Crumb did for comics.

They seemed like they would be best buddies in the way they shared their artwork with one another. Bakshi would show Crumb some of his drawings and ideas for which Crumb would lend him his sketchbook of various characters. But Crumb was weary of Bakshi's idea to adapt his beloved comic book character into a feature film. Despite remaining rather faithful to the source material (practically word-for-word in many scenes), Crumb did not want to sign the contracts because of his own worries.

The film would never have been made if it wasn't for Crumb's wife Dana signing the contracts with her power of attorney. How did Crumb react to the film? He killed off Fritz in his comic promptly with a jealous girlfriend stabbing him in the back. It was a shocking turn of events that was later referenced in Bakshi's *Wizards* (1977) when an idiot soldier remarks "They killed Fritz!" after accidentally shooting his comrade. For what it's worth, Bakshi's *Fritz the Cat* did inspire me to pick up some of Crumb's archival comic book works which were some of the most evocatively surreal illustrations I've ever read.

But even after acquiring the rights, Bakshi still had to climb the mountain of funding. Convincing studio executives to help produce an animated feature outside of Disney was a monumental task, let alone the first X-rated animated feature. He somehow managed to convince Warner Brothers to get in on it, but they soon pulled funding after their jaws dropped upon witnessing the work in progress. It was naturally a better fit when Cinemation Industries decided to pick up the project given their fondness for producing grindhouse and exploitation pictures.

Lifted directly from elements of the comic, the film gives us an exaggerated and anthropomorphized vision of the 1960's. Bakshi introduces the film's decade with his voice describing it as a happy and heavy time. The first shot says it all with a group of construction workers having their lunch on scaffolding, ranting and discussing the changing times they do not agree with.

During the conversation about one of their daughters living with some guy in college, a worker gets up to pull out his comically oversized penis and urinates down below on a passing hippie. This scene sets the tone for the entire picture. It's an animated film about a time of revolution, but doesn't sugar coat any of its ignorance or vulgarity. Driving home this point is how the opening credits appear entirely over descending urine.

We first spot our feline protagonist Fritz, dressed societally acceptable in a red sweater and no pants, wandering Central Park for women among a crowd of guitar players. His ear catches three women fawning over a silent black man (portrayed in this universe as a crow), speaking about how they're all for black power and discussing their vision of racism in society ("Why does a great actor like James Earl Jones always have to play black men?").

After the black crow laughs at their ignorance in trying to be progressive, Fritz feeds the women the intellectual drivel that they want to hear. Throwing himself all over the street as a tortured soul, he lures the three of them into an apartment for an orgy. But with a packed house of potheads, it isn't long before the orgy grows comically large. The potheads feed the girls more intellectual nonsense as they copulate and smoke weed.

Meanwhile, two bumbling pig cops squabble and argue outside their door before staging a raid. One of the cops, perfectly voiced by Ralph Bakshi himself, is particularly protective about his Jewish nature. A Jewish pig just sounded too wild for Bakshi to pass up. After some comical back and forth between the two, they bust in and proceed with beating up the naked hippies until there is a mountain of unconscious drugged up kids. Fritz, still in a trippy stupor, grabs the cop's gun and shoots the toilet. The overflowing water causes a flood in the apartment allowing Frtiz an exit from the situation.

For the rest of the film, Fritz is on the run from the cops while indulging his fantasies and political beliefs. He goes off on his roommates for wasting their lives and accidentally burns down the entire student dorm complex. He walks the ghetto neighborhoods of black crows hoping he can be seen as a cool cat that's down with the revolution. He incites a violent riot for the poor black folks to rise up and kill the rich. And, in his darkest moment of realization, he teams up with a group of dangerous neo-Nazis and masochists that aim to blow up a power plant.

The journey of Fritz is a strange one with many outlandish detours. While hanging with a crow, he catches the attention of a seductive female crow with a chubby yet toned body (a female figure Crumb favored most in his comics as a fetish). Fritz goes on a drug trip as the stripping female crow leads him on into a strange sexual chase through a junkyard. Midway through intercourse, he becomes inspired to start a cultural revolution and rushes off to rally the people. Police get involved with the revolt and it ends with a bloody shootout in the streets - exaggerated to the point where jets are called in to bomb Harlem. Fritz does not witness the death of his Harlem pal who dies slowly in a metaphor of pool balls signaling the countdown of his demise. He merely shouts "We shall overcome!" from behind an alley and scurries off as a pig cop is brutally gunned down by a crow sniper.

There are many small bits of exaggeration that are so brief and comical I found myself rewinding several times on my first viewing. While trying to appear cool in front of the crows, Fritz steals a car to go on a joyride and impress his new black friend. He zooms through an alley and swipes by a trash can. A crow pops out of the trash can to inject himself with a needle as he gets the shivers and sinks back into the can. Look just to the left in that same scene and you'll see a crow hanging laundry out to dry from her window, become tangled in the line and plummet to the street naked. As Fritz continues driving dangerously, he causes a milk truck to crash that spills out piles of drugs instead of its intended cargo. These details give the film not only a snappy sense of a humor, but also provide some brilliant satire of the era.

As his first animated feature film, you can see the beginnings of Bakshi's trademarks. Desiring to make his animated characters feel both alive and believable, he recorded dialogue right on the streets of New York. His recording methods were a sound engineer's nightmare, but this was an important element Bakshi wanted. The natural and unscripted voices, while vastly different in quality from many of the professionally recorded sequences, does deliver a sense of reality.

The scene of a Harlem bar focuses entirely on three black crows sitting at a table. They don't talk about anything in particular, mostly lamenting with laughs about their childhood. The scene serves no purpose to the plot other than establishing the setting through its people in the background. The voices are that of real black patrons in a Harlem bar who Bakshi hung out with and asked questions over drinks while he recorded. Bakshi doesn't just want to animate a caricature of New York - he wants the city to sing with its own voice in addition to his own.

The cult phenomenon of *Fritz* launched a new wave of adult

animated pictures. A sequel was quickly commissioned, *The Nine Lives of Fritz the Cat* (1974), but was not directed by Bakshi as he wanted to create more original animated films. Directing duties were turned over to *Fritz the Cat* animator Robert Taylor. Though the film didn't meet the approval of Bakshi or Crumb, it did become the first animated film to be officially selected for the Cannes Film Festival. The most shameless of cash-ins was the animated film *Dirty Duck* (1974) which was quickly denounced for being so uninspired with its crude content and lackluster design. While Bakshi's style of adult animation certainly wasn't lightning in a bottle, the irreverent nature of *Fritz the Cat* certainly was something that could never be duplicated successfully.

Fritz the Cat was the first animated film I watched when I attended college in the fall of 2004. In the final days of a hyped presidential campaign and trying to adjust to the environment of downtown Minneapolis, I found myself very confused and unsure of what to expect from this completely new avenue of knowledge. Watching *Fritz the Cat* gave me an idea of the wild and untamed nature that youth aspires towards, playfully lampooned with its own style.

Though dated in its subject matter, it contains nuggets of hilarious perspective that let me know the world may be corrupt and unkind, but also that you can still find some humor and love in all that danger (warped though it may be). It was that odd reassurance I needed to venture out and explore the new world I'd have to live in. It may sound strange to bestow that praise on an animated film featuring a cat having sex with a crow, but what can I tell you? The strangest things keep us going in life and Bakshi's *Fritz the Cat* is a blunt animated piece of brilliance that just happens to be one of them.

GHOST IN THE SHELL

The world of *Ghost in the Shell* (1995) is a dense futuristic environment of towering skyscrapers and ever-evolving technology. Most cyberpunk or science fiction tales of future tech tend to focus on either one or two major innovations that change society in a few specific ways. *Ghost in the Shell* opens up a massive can of worms by developing a world accepting of cybernetic augmentation with online communication in your brain. It presents a fear of robotization, but from a more philosophical standpoint that it cannot be stopped. Cyborgs are commonplace for the human population which results in a restructuring of national security. It's much harder to keep tabs on other people when they can easily swap out bodies and minds as if they were car parts.

Handling most of these tricky crimes is the government organization Section 9. Leading officer Motoko Kusanagi is the most hands-on of the group, exposing her nude form to don a stealth mode and take on dangerous missions with gun in hand. In her opening scene atop a skyscraper, Motoko removes her clothes, drops down several floors with a cable, assassinates her target through the window and then disappears into the night sky with a special type of technological camouflage. One thing to notice about Motoko's body is that her nudity doesn't appear sexual. There is coldness to her artificial body that seems to have more in common with a plastic doll than a human form.

The opening credits reveal the intricate origins in assembling Motoko's body. Her muscles and skeletal system are laid bare as her brain is encased in its technological cage. Chemicals coat and form around her remaining figure to form the rest of the inorganic elements. It's the strange nature of how Motoko has become a stronger cop and less of a human. Her brain now locked in a cybernetic body has made her perceive the world much differently.

Basic senses become distant echoes and you can't help but wonder how the inorganic female form signifies a death of humanity without the means of reproduction.

This theme plays in with the latest target for Section 9, an elusive suspect known as the Puppet Master. Existing as a sentient form of life that has taken hold of cyborg bodies, the Puppet Master seeks the next evolutionary jump for its new race. It wants to merge and breed, to possess human abilities and expand past a singular miracle of the digital revolution. The sentient lifeform has a need to survive and evolve as its own species. This is either the replacement or evolution for humanity, spawning from the data and circuitries of its creators.

In addition to the fear of the robotization of society, there is also a fear of losing women. Aside from the obvious observation of Motoko's inability to menstruate with a cyborg body, there's a definite loss of humanity and femininity in her current state. What exactly separates Motoko's female cyborg body from that of a male cyborg aside from the inclusion of functionless breasts? It's that sense of uniformity which may make her an equal player in battles both technological and physical, but robs her of individuality.

The occupation of a cyborg body for so long has made this woman cold and emotionless towards the world and her body. Take a look at the climactic finale where a nude Motoko jumps on top of a spider tank and tries to force open the hatch. The muscles in her arms pulsate and stretch as the force of the pulling begins to rip her at the seams. Synthetic skin and circuitry begin to pull apart from her body until she loses both her limbs.

The tank swings around to brush her off the top and then grabs her head with a claw. As the claw starts to crush Motoko's head, she appears lifeless as a doll. Her eyes are dead, her expression is blank and her voice is silenced. She is damaged and on the verge of death without proper functions to express pain. Is she feeling anything as her skull is about to be crushed or has that sensation been damaged?

After she is rescued by her male partner Batou, her body lying damaged and emotionless on the ground, Motoko seems to speak clearly and calmly through her cybernetic brain. She seems so unnerved by her physical altercation that she demands to dive into the cyber-brain of her target in her current state with no arms or clothing.

Director Mamoru Oshii makes perhaps one of the most earnest

attempts at delivering deeper science fiction to the mainstream. The dialogue goes on for long stretches of theories and concerns about the psychology behind technological advancement, but the passages are sandwiched in between moments of intense action. Before questioning a memory-wiped pawn of the Puppet Master, we witness a running and gunning chase through the busy nooks of Hong Kong. Before proceeding into an intricate analysis of procreation being a key element to immortality, the audience is treated to a brilliantly staged battle of female cyborg versus spider-like tank. A spoonful of action helps the philosophy go down.

Taking place in a highly detailed vision of a futuristic Hong Kong that isn't too clean or flashy, Oshii allows the viewer to enjoy all the little details of this environment. There is a breathing moment for Motoko when she observes her exterior surroundings while taking a ride on a boat. No distinguishable dialogue can be heard and the soundtrack takes over with a powerful choir and drums. A plane passes dangerously close to the city, casting its large shadow over the populace. The flashing traffic lights can be seen from a bridge as we pass under it. A gaggle of girls don their yellow umbrellas as the rain begins to pour down on the city streets.

These may seem like nothing moments that do little more than show off the impressive animation, but they're very necessary for a movie such as this. Between all the perplexing theories and barrage of bullets traded in every scene, a quiet moment of observation comes as a welcomed break from the action.

As security forces scramble to stop a car full of criminals, the soundtrack drops for a sitar track as we watch helicopters whirl around skyscrapers and ground forces set up barricades in the middle of a rainy highway. Little details are focused on from the tiniest water droplets to the brightest overhead lights of the highway tunnels. These features display a world that is real and believable as opposed to a future splattered with too much tech that is overly shiny and somewhat useless.

The film was certainly ahead of its time both in technological speculation and sci-fi storytelling. It is often marked as the key inspiration behind the Wachowski's action touchstone *The Matrix* (1999). Compare the changing structures of human beings in those two films. In *The Matrix*, the rebellious humans tap into the robots' programmable world via inputs on the back of their necks. In *Ghost in the Shell*, all cyborgs come standard with neck inputs that allow them to plug into the net and connect more freely with other servers and systems. While pursuing a suspect in a car with her partner, Motoko sits in the passenger seat connecting to the traffic networks while at the same driving the car electronically. Her driving partner sits there in amazement as she is able to multitask while completely still.

There is also a questioning of reality at every turn when everything you see and hear is through a digital component. One of the suspects that Section 9 brings in for questioning is a garbage man unwittingly helping a cybercriminal by tapping into street phones. The garbage man is doing it for the cash so he can be closer to his daughter after he divorced his wife. But he was being played more than he thought as his memories have been tampered with. He never had a daughter or a wife. The picture of his daughter that he treasures was actually a photo of himself with his dog. He tears up in the interrogation room when detectives break the news that it may be impossible to recover his original memories.

Directly following this scene, we see Motoko underwater, staring up at her reflection on the surface of the water. After rising to the surface and grabbing a beer on Batou's boat, she relays the experience as a meeting of her former self that was more human than machine. It's a nostalgic moment for the days when you didn't have to worry about your mind and body being tampered with by unseen forces. In the same way that *The Matrix* questions whether what you are experiencing right now is not just a computer program, *Ghost in the Shell* presents a fear that such a theory is not so strange for the not so distant future of technology.

The animation of *Ghost in the Shell* was very unique for its time, utilizing a process dubbed DGA (Digitally Generated Animation). Both traditional and digital cel art was combined into the final frame along with CGI. You can see this animation shine in many of the deep shots of the city. The best example is when Motoko ride a boat through a canal and under a bridge. You can sense a detailed depth of field from the way the bridge appears close and clear while the skyscrapers in the background appear more hazy and blurry.

Oshii returned to direct the sequel *Ghost in the Shell 2: Innocence* (2004) with just as many fresh ideas as he had with the first film (perhaps more). The story followed Batou as the main character and the color palette had shifted from cool to warm tones. Inspirations for *Innocence* included the dolls of Hans Bellmer and a recommendation by Jean-Luc Godard to include author quotes into the dialogue and texts on screen. Challenging and mesmerizingly different from its predecessor, *Innocence* was a fantastic follow up that garnered more acclaim and made it the sixth animated film ever accepted into the Cannes Film Festival.

Ghost in the Shell was later updated by Mamoru Oshii in 2010 as *Ghost in the Shell 2.0* (not to be confused with the actual sequel). In this special cut, he adds some new computer graphics to a handful of scenes and a warmer color palette to reflect the colors he used in the sequel. He more or less pulled what George Lucas did with the remastered editions of the *Star Wars* trilogy. While Oshii's 2.0 cut doesn't drastically change the story, it feels unneeded. I will admit that he does improve on the CGI of the radar shots which appear more like something out of *Tron* in the original cut.

While not as close to its source material of the comic books, Oshii's *Ghost in the Shell* dares to be more visually intricate and philosophically deeper. It's a science fiction classic that has been saddled alongside *Blade Runner* as the most inspirational of the genre in both story and design. Brimming with ideas and oozing with detail, it's exactly how I like my science fiction served.

GRAVE OF THE FIREFLIES

Grave of the Fireflies (1988) is not a traditional film about war. There are no scenes of soldiers in combat. There are no sights of exploding planes or boats assaulted by gunfire. And, probably the most important aspect, we never see much of the assaulting American forces that bomb Japan. The prime focus is on the Japanese families that run in terror from their bombed towns and cities. It's a rare breed of a war picture that attempts to humanize more than demonize.

The film focuses on the firebombing of a Japanese village in which teenage boy Seita barely escapes the horrific attack with his little sister Setsuko. In the aftermath, they find their mother badly burned and a few inches from death at a recovery center. Their father is unseen as he is currently serving in the armed forces. Fed up with the food rationing of their spiteful aunt, the two decide to live on their own in the country - sleeping in an old mineshaft and stealing from farmers.

Grave of the Fireflies is so effective in its shock and tears that nothing can prepare you for that big moment of sadness. The film even begins with the spoiler of Seita lying dead in a train station, relaying that this is the story of how he dies. We know this will not end well. But even with that prior knowledge, the film still broke my heart with all the joy and adversity that leads up to the demise of Seita and his sister Setsuko.

Many critics have often cited the film's animation for inspiring the largest levels of humanity in the medium. To tell the truth, the animation style of *Fireflies* doesn't appear all that divergent from the a-typical anime design formula. Characters appear with massive eyes that are so large they seem to occupy the same dimensions as dinner plates. Several anime productions adopt the similar technique of displaying more emotion through the windows to the soul, inspired from Disney's exaggerations and expanded by Japanese artists to absurd degrees.

But what's perhaps the biggest achievement to the animation is the aspect of exaggeration that never overshadows the humanity. The emotions never feel artificial and you lose yourself in the characters and their situations. This isn't so much about how the animation looks, but how it is used. There are plenty of moments where very simple actions of reality appear beautifully animated with attention to seemingly minute details. Seita sits in a bath holding a washcloth under the water to create an air bubble and unleashes it in Setsuko's surprised face. Seita cleans himself off with a towel in a field, rubbing his head and wiping his face. These are simple moments where nothing all that interesting happens except a believability of humanity.

This is the type of film that could not work as well in live-action, though two directors have tried since. That's certainly what author Ariyuki Nosaka thought when his semi-autobiographical short story was to be adapted to film. His primary concern was that child actors would not be able to correctly convey the characters he wrote. But when offered the opportunity to adapt his story to animation, Nosaka was surprised at how well his story could appear on screen. After viewing the storyboards and marveling at their accuracy in the setting, Nosaka came to the ultimate conclusion that animation was the only sufficient medium for his story.

There's a very soft quality to the animation that gives it a heavier tone of realism. Several of the illustrative outlines were drawn in brown as opposed to the customary black. Color coordinator Michiyo Yasuda found it more difficult using brown as it didn't contrast as well and had never been done before in Japanese animation. There were other challenging ideas for the animation, but a strict schedule didn't allow much time for experimentation.

Director Isao Takahata's involvement mostly sprung from his interest in holding up youth higher than soldiers in wartime. He was drawn to the character of Seita who attempts to be committed to the survival and well-being of his sister Setsuko. But it was Setsuko that presented an interesting challenge to the director in that he had never depicted a four-year-old girl. Setsuko is a very interesting character in the aspect of her mannerism and evolving mental state. She is not as collected as her big brother in that she will often cry or become frustrated over things she doesn't fully comprehend.

When refused to see her dying mother, Setsuko goes silent as she stares at the ground. Seita attempts to shift the conversation gently to staying at their aunt's house and offering his sister food rations, but Setsuko continues to stare at the ground as she shuffles her feet and says with the slightest pout that she wants to see mama. Seita calmly states that it's too late to see her at the moment as Setsuko's tears slowly begin to flow. There are several tough moments such as this where Setsuko becomes a real little girl who longs for her mother and not just a cartoon character trying to fit the role.

The simplest of her actions create the sense of a real little girl. She bawls in bed from a nightmare as she kicks and flails her arms with her eyes still closed. She jumps in delight when Seita fills her empty candy tin with water, stomping her feet with her hands out to get a chance to shake the tin. There's even an independent side as she appears focused and determined when helping Seita cook a meal. As a father of a little girl, these scenes ring all too true of how a four-year-old girl would act. To see that realism in an animated character and then watch them suffer the cruel fate of living in a time of war creates a harsh reality.

There comes a very depressing moment in the picture when Setsuko stops crying after coming to terms with her mother's death. It is then that Seita begins to cry realizing he couldn't protect Setsuko's innocence. As Setsuko slowly grows worse from starvation, we watch her body lose muscle and her spirit grow weak as she attempts to remain strong.

And then comes the ultimate tear-jerking moment - the event dreaded since the beginning of the film. Setsuko does not wake up. Seita sleeps next to her body through the night and gives her a proper funeral in the morning. The scene then cuts to bittersweet music with animation of Setsuko playing by the mineshaft alone. This is the most powerful scene in the entire film as it reminds us that Setsuko was just a little girl, filled with curiosity, playfulness, creativity and bravery. Her future is ripped away and it's gut-wrenching to comprehend such a tragedy befalling a real little girl.

Despite the opinions of critics that the film is anti-war, Takahata insists that this is not the case. His primary goal was to evoke sympathy for a brother and sister who have failed in trying to be independent. He was successful in that Seita and Setsuko are built up to be so human that watching them suffer hurt me to the point of tears.

An old girlfriend from college once burst into my dorm room in a downer mood, demanding to watch a sad movie. Having seen many, I asked her to what level of sadness she was in the mood for. She inclined that she wanted the saddest movie I had to offer. I told her about *Grave of the Fireflies* ahead of popping it in the DVD player and she still wanted to see it. By the time we reached the tearful overture of the little girl soon after her demise, she had placed a pond of tears on my shoulder. I have never seen a woman cry so hard and so much over an animated feature film. I can only imagine how weepy an entire theater audience may have been when witnessing the saddest thing you may ever see drawn for the screen.

HEAVY TRAFFIC

The first time I watched *Heavy Traffic* (1973) was within the student lounge at college in 2005. Between classes I'd often check out a film from the library and play it on the lounge television - a worn piece of educational equipment from the 1990's. Having previously seen Ralph Bakshi's *Fritz the Cat*, I had an idea of the style that he'd bring to this off-beat feature of an aspiring cartoonist in an inner-city setting.

Everyone else in the lounge did not know what to expect. For many, this was their first experience with the peculiar works of Ralph Bakshi's adult animated films. Wild with vulgarity and never pulling a punch, the film soon bred a crowd that grew by the minute. We laughed hard and uncomfortably at the brutal honesty and caricature on screen. I can recall the scene of a crucified Jesus Christ blabbing to a mafia godfather about black people touching his olive oil was met with a big response of uneasy laughter. By the time the film had ended, there was a large audience inhabiting the room that was still reeling from the trip. The next round of classes had just been dismissed and more students piled into the lounge trying to figure out why we're all so gathered and talkative around the TV. We started up the film from the beginning and let them know why.

The infatuation of *Heavy Traffic* comes from Bakshi's brain bluntly splattered all over the drawings. He doesn't leave anything out of the film's urban microcosm. As the theatrical trailer describes it best, "You'll meet hoods, hustlers, freaks, creeps, cops, crazies, weirdos, whinos, hard-heads, low-lifes and God."

The film opens with live-action footage of the bowler hat wearing, 24-year-old Michael playing pinball at the arcade. As he continues the monotony of clicking flippers and pulling springs, we hear his random thoughts about society ("What do you see...Where does it all go...Who do you screw?"). Michael's thoughts begin to take the form of animation. While continuing his mental questioning and ranting, we see his cartoonish view of society. An angered man on the street pistol whips a nearby gentleman and proceeds to rape his girlfriend. A pimp pays off some crooked cops who soon deliver a beating towards a homeless man. A police officer attempts to help a woman on a high ledge, but she spits in his face just to watch him slam on the street below.

Aside from the local color of a corrupt inner-city environment, Bakshi breathes both reality and cartoonish satire into the characters. Michael's mother, Ida, and his father, Angelo, are constantly going at each other's throats with his dad an Italian mobster and his mom a viciously protective Jew. Not only do they bicker about how to raise their adult son, but they furiously try to kill each other. While they beat each other senseless in the background, Michael finds himself engrossed in his drawings. Born from his home life, one cartoon reflects a married couple beating one another with their genitals and breasts.

Throughout the picture we get to know all the colorful characters of Michael's neighborhood. Crazy Moe babbles and laments on an apartment roof about growing old in between his desire to kill a pigeon. Snowflake, a sassy transvestite hooker, picks up a male construction worker only to be savagely beaten when he discovers his date has an erection. Shorty, a legless and surly bar patron, defends Snowflake with his buff arms and platform of wheels. All of these characters become so unique and interesting that the film will often veer off into different situations with them.

The one character Michael sticks to throughout the picture is Carole, his black sweetheart of a bartender. Tired of taking crap from her boss, she quits her job and shacks up with Michael. When life becomes too hectic at home, Michael and Carole hit the streets to make a living on their own. Michael attempts to sell some of his underground cartoons to an animation mogul that is shocked and appalled at Michael's illustrations of Jesus shooting God in the face. Life begins to take strange and dark turns as Michael and Carole struggle for money.

Certain scenes become uncomfortable to watch, but with a mixed tone. In the scene where Snowflake is beaten by a construction worker, the transvestite flies around the bar after every punch as if he were a *Looney Tunes* character. He laughs as he soars through the air and floats to the ground while the angry construction worker calls him a fag, mercilessly delivering a pounding. It's not until the last shot of the fight where Snowflake is beaten and bloody does the reality sink in and Shorty comes to save the day.

There are also scenes where so much is going on you're not sure what to feel. Angelo returns home with the obese Rosa in hopes of getting his son laid. While Rosa forces sex on Michael with her grotesque naked figure, Angelo and Ida violently fight on the fire escape over what to do about their son. It's probably one of the most awkward scenes of any animated movie I've seen where you're not sure whether to laugh or wince at what transpires.

Heavy Traffic is one of Ralph Bakshi's most defining pictures as it establishes both his original style and personal storytelling. Characters mostly appear designed with long faces and large mouths dripping off their faces. Similar to how he recorded the raw dialogue of *Fritz the Cat*, Bakshi allows the actors to play it loose in front of the microphone. Ad-libbing was encouraged to the point where Bakshi could sense a natural flow to the voice. He wanted his animation to maintain that sense of realism of society while at the same time satirizing it. You can actually hear Bakshi's voice in most of the background dialogue.

Beats in the story are punctuated by pings and prods of a pinball machine, relating to the arbitrary luck of life. Sometimes your life hits the jackpot and other times it's slammed into a bumper. The inspiration for this came from Bakshi's days spent in penny arcades playing pinball while pondering life. Whoever said those games were just a waste of coins?

Bakshi used live-action footage for this picture in a number of ways. He uses it straight as with the bookend scenes of Michael playing pinball. He uses it for the backgrounds in the form of still photographs of real locations. He alters the contrast of live-action female models to deliver some strangely creepy scenes as with the backgrounds at a garment business. Old stock footage of stage acts are utilized to serve as the background for a night club. Bakshi would use live-action much more in his future films for the rotoscoped animation of *Wizards* (1977), *The Lord of the Rings* (1978) and *American Pop* (1981), but Bakshi admitted that he hated using it as it was merely a means of keeping production costs low.

While Bakshi intended for *Heavy Traffic* to be his first animated film, producer Steve Krantz suggested that executives wouldn't go along with it for both Bakshi's inexperience and the adult nature of the content. After he completed *Fritz the Cat* which was met with financial success, Bakshi was able to produce *Heavy Traffic* after pitching it to producer Samuel Z. Arkoff. Though both Krantz and Arkoff were producers on *Heavy Traffic*, Krantz became a major pain in the butt for Bakshi. It was halfway through production on the film and Krantz still hadn't paid Bakshi what he was owed on *Fritz the Cat*. He told Bakshi the film didn't make any money, but that argument didn't seem to hold water after Krantz purchased a BMW and a mansion.

And it only got worse as Bakshi began the process of seeking a producer for his next film, *Coonskin* (1975). Krantz was so angered that Bakshi wouldn't talk about his next film with him that he locked Bakshi out of the studio. He even started looking for replacement directors such as Chuck Jones (I can't even imagine how Chuck would approach such material). Arkoff ultimately came to the rescue by threatening to pull funding if Bakshi wasn't allowed to direct the picture.

Just as with *Fritz the Cat*, an X rating was given to *Heavy Traffic*. Krantz had attempted to trim down the adult content for an R rating, but the X rating is what the film received. However, because of the acclaim and box office that Bakshi had built up with his first film, *Heavy Traffic* received a larger theatrical release than *Fritz the Cat*. Not only did the film do well financially, but it also received an abundance of critical praise. Film critic Vincent Canby of The New York Times placed the film on his list of the "Ten Best Films of 1973".

Bakshi's *Heavy Traffic* represents the animation director at his best with a fearless story and animation that was boldly experimental. Even after the game-changing *Fritz the Cat*, the director still found a way to break new ground with topics and imagery that were shockingly refreshing for a handcuffed medium. The trailer still sums it up best: "It's animated, but it's not a cartoon. It's funny, but it's not a comedy. It's real, it's unreal, it's heavy."

THE INCREDIBLES

It is midnight on a Monday in 2005. My roommate and I have just finished walking back to our dorm after a long day of studies. We are both exhausted. When we finally open the door and seem to be ready to hit the hay, a thought pops into my roommate's head. He asks if I want to watch *The Incredibles* (2004). We had both already seen the film a dozen times since it had been released on home video, but I just could not bring myself to say no. We both had classes early the next morning, but did not care.

We loved this film so much that we just had to watch it again at such an absurd time. That, to me, is the mark of a great film - one that makes you stays up into the late-night hours just because you have to see it one more time. If my roommate burst into my room at 3am to ask me again, I'm afraid I would agree to another viewing.

Pixar's *The Incredibles* is one of their best and not just because it's an animated action film more appealing for adults. It presents a true sense of unparalleled family and character. The superhero adults of this universe first appear in the prime of their lives. They hop and skip around a vivid metropolis, stopping bad guys and making small talk with other heroes as if they were students passing each other in the hallway.

Soon after many of the heroes become married, the government shuts down their vigilantism and forces them to assume simple lives. Bob is reduced from a crime stopper with super strength to a mere pencil pusher at an insurance agency. The bulky employee is tightly packed in a small cubicle where he drearily does his best to file paperwork and speak with clients. The spark of enthusiasm he displayed in the opening is all but diminished.

His wife Helen appears less phased to hang up her Elasti-Girl costume. She appreciates a life less dangerous to spend time with her family of three children. The kids, however, favor more of Bob's mentality. They feel held back in their abilities and what's expected of them. Dash, the middle child, has energy to spare with his super speed. It frustrates him endlessly that he can't show off his abilities in sports. Violet is a quiet and shy girl who finds herself using her powers of invisibility to hide from others (despite her clothes not disappearing with her body). Jack-Jack, the baby, is just untapped potential that is later revealed as a cavalcade of different abilities. All of these elements combine to form a story that can both have fun with the elements of superhero stories and take aim at the frustrations of uniformity.

If you think I'm reading too much into this then you should see some of the theories online comparing Bob's boiling frustration of lowering the bar to that of Ayn Rand's fearful philosophy. This may seem even more apparent when the villain Syndrome reveals his evil scheme for restructuring the post-superhero world ("...when everyone's super, no one will be"). But director Brad Bird spelled it out clearly that he has no political bias and finds himself more as a centralist laughing at both sides of the aisle. He's more concerned with telling a fun and relatable story than injecting some political message into his work.

What Bird does bring to this script is a believable sense of family amid their teamwork to take down an evil villain. There are a lot of personal touches to the film the way Bird relates to the tough decisions for his family during the 1990's concerning his career. Drawing from that inspiration, he creates characters that are both relatable and infatuating. You can spot this element in the way Bob appears lost during dinner and the way Helen has a critical eye when she catches her figure in a mirror.

In the casting of the voices, Pixar went more for the apt voices rather than the ones with marquee value. Craig T. Nelson and Holly Hunter were not exactly big names at the time, but they blended seamlessly into the roles of Bob and Helen Incredible. Sarah Vowell is better known as a writer of American history and a commentator on National Public Radio, but she lends her voice well to the role of the awkward teenager Violet. Bud Luckey, Pixar's character designing elder, provides the grizzled voice of government agent Rick Dicker, the man in charge of relocating superheroes.

Even Brad Bird himself jumps into the picture, voicing the tiny fashion designer Edna Mode. With his nasally delivery a designer both snobby and perky, Bird helps the story move along by addressing the superhero costumes with smart humor and energy. When Bob meets with her to discuss a new design for his outfit, Edna pushes him away from capes with many examples of superheroes meeting their end thanks to an unfortunate choice in fashion.

True to the character of Edna, Brad Bird was one of the most vocal and passionate of directors Pixar ever had. Arguments would often break out during the production process and Bird strived for maximum potential out of everything. Behind the scenes footage reveals a heated exchange over the design of Bob. If he wasn't getting what he wanted or something wasn't working, he made sure you knew it. If you weren't speaking up, he made sure to raise your volume. Bird would often single out Tony Fucile for being so quiet and mumbling his words during meetings. One staff member playfully wrote a song with his guitar about Bird that he titled The 800 Pound Gorilla with lyrics citing how he would scream in the morning. Producer John Walker told Bird in a meeting that he was just trying to push him towards the finish line to which Bird argued that he wanted to get across the finish line in first place.

Bird's quest for perfection was very much warranted given how this production would be the most challenging of Pixar's features at the time. *Finding Nemo* had roughly 22 environments whereas *The Incredibles* had over 130 of them. The human characters would have to age, grow and change clothing rather than remain a consistent shape. The effects would be more demanding as an action picture that featured car chases, city-smashing robots, jet-destroying missiles and a volcanic paradise. While other Pixar films relied on a sense of matching reality, *The Incredibles* would push the characters to not only look and act human, but also possess super-strength and stretch their bodies with the right amount of weight and proportions. But thanks to the tireless efforts of everyone involved, coupled with Bird's pushing for more out of the studio, *The Incredibles* appears surprisingly natural for having such a massive laundry list of requirements.

Animation buffs will take note of the climactic battle featuring cameos by veteran animators Frank Thomas and Ollie Johnston, two of the illustrious Nine Old Men of Disney. They previously had a small cameo in Brad Bird's *The Iron Giant*, but with *The Incredibles* they are given a more telling and fitting role. When the Incredible family gathers around the destroyed robot as bystanders cheer, Frank and Ollie appear off to the side commenting on how that fight was old school ("No school like the old school"). For animators and animation enthusiasts, their presence and dialogue signals an acceptance of CGI as an art form - an assurance that quality animation will continue into the 21st century.

During the 1980's, Brad Bird worked with some of his animator friends to create a pencil test for adapting classic comic book hero The Spirit into an animated feature. Nobody seemed interested in creating an animated feature about superheroes with a more adult mentality to stories of action and adventure. Brad Bird not only proved that you could make such a concept work for animation, but that you could also give it a sense of heart and family.

In the audio commentary for the *The Incredibles*, Bird argues that animation is an art form and not a genre. If someone asks him what it's like working in the animation genre, he angrily said he'd punch that person. I'm fairly sure I have not referred to animation as a genre in this book. If I have made that mistake, please, not in the face, Mr. Bird.

THE IRON GIANT

If an animated film made in the 1990's wasn't produced by Disney, it had a large uphill battle with rising standards. The new wave of Disney animated features such as *The Little Mermaid* (1989), *Beauty and The Beast* (1991) and *Aladdin* (1992) pushed the bar so far up that anything even slightly below that stellar quality was seen as not good enough. Animated films such as *Thumbelina* (1994), *The Swan Princess* (1994) and *Quest for Camelot* (1998) did not impress audiences or critics alike which led to the predictable scoffing of Disney being better (which, to be honest, they most often were). The critical and financial disapproval led to Warner Brothers cutting back severely on their feature animation division. Such cuts, however, led to director Brad Bird being allowed the freedom to craft *The Iron Giant* (1999) as one of the few shining stars amid Disney's animation grip on the decade.

When British poet Ted Hughes wrote his 1968 novel *The Iron Man*, I doubt he imagined it'd be turned into a theatrical animated feature (especially in a market that was crowded with upbeat musicals). It did, however, have a rock opera helmed by Pete Townshend in the 1980's. When Warner Brothers acquired the rights to the book in 1994, they weren't too sure how to proceed with the animated adaptation initially. They placed their faith in director Brad Bird, known at the time for his directorial efforts on *The Simpsons*. Bird adored the book and saw that there was a rich enough mythology to such a tale that could be weaved into something relatable and brilliant.

There's a lot to love in the characters Bird establishes for the 1950's setting of this film. Our protagonist is a plucky all-American boy, Hogarth Hughes, who encapsulates everything fun about being a kid. While his single mother works late shifts at the diner, he spends his evenings with trashy science fiction on the television and whipped cream injected Twinkies (according to Brad Bird, it's called a Turbo-Twinkie). He does his best to maintain his cool composure in front of the local beatnik/junkyard owner Dean. But it's rather hard for him to contain both his fear and excitement when a giant robot wanders into his humble little town.

The titular giant is a gentle soul encased in iron. Crashing down on Earth, he has no memory of who he is or where he came from. Curious and confused, the giant befriends Hogarth as his friend, teacher and concealer of his identity. Hogarth brings him home to hide in the barn and shows off his favorite comic book characters, stating how the giant should strive to be someone cool and heroic as Superman. The boy bestows all his accumulated knowledge of humanity to the giant, explaining why he should keep out of sight until people are ready to accept him. There's an exceptionally tender moment when the giant happens upon a shot deer in which Hogarth talks about death. It's quite a scene to see a child try to comprehend such a subject and teach it to someone else.

The giant was rendered in CGI and with a fairly simple design, but comes off as a believable character in a world of traditionally drawn human characters. With his underbite jaw and headlight eyes, he's surprisingly capable of many emotional states, even with his limited facial expressions. It's mostly his body language that communicates his status so well. When depressed, the giant lies in a junkyard repeatedly lifting a car hood with his finger and letting it fall down. When frightened about being discovered, the giant's eyes go wide as he quickly looks in every direction for a place to conceal himself. The perfect amount of computer texturing allows the computer-rendered giant to blend in smoothly with the 2D medium. Any scene where the giant holds Hogarth to either give him a ride or protect him is amazingly fluid in the seamless combination of both a hand-drawn character and a CGI character.

The presence of the giant frightens the townsfolk so much that they call the government to send someone to investigate. Kent Mansley, a cocky and short-fused government agent, is sent to track down this mysterious creature. Shocked and intrigued by the evidence of chomped vehicles from the giant's appetite for metal, Kent feverishly proceeds with his investigation by tracking Hogarth as a suspected witness. He's a great villain who uses his atomic age hysteria to stir up the military. His voice cracks whenever he spots the giant as he jumps up and down pointing at the metal monster while screaming for soldiers to fire. He's equal parts funny and creepy in his desire to ascend the ladder in Washington.

I love the look and design of the 1950's Maine setting that embodies a Norman Rockwell sense of charm. Characters will appear with the slightest blush to their faces and the softest of shadows. The use of colors common to the era sets the right tone and tells us more about the time than forcing in references. There could have been no mention of Sputnik 1 or the *Duck and Cover* educational films and you'd still be able to recognize it as the 1950's. Even the design of the giant when he goes into defensive mode still carries a 1950's vibe as a robot you might see in a comic book or a cheesy sci-fi movie of that decade. His abundance of lasers and spider-like weaponry has an impressive *War of the Worlds* touch.

The production of *The Iron Giant* is a prime example of how creative control trumps budget and schedule. As a tradeoff, Warner Brothers mostly left Brad Bird and his team alone as long as they were making progress for not having the same time and money as a Disney or DreamWorks production. The amazing results were a combination of Bird's commitment to planning, the use of new software and the reliance on the creative forces of his team. Bird would spread out his animation team and give them various scenes to work on rather than have them be regulated to one character or types of shots.

Bird would also be open to any new ideas that could improve the movie as was the case with storyboard artist Teddy Newton. Teddy had an unusual amount of freedom that allowed him to conceive wild new directions for the story. His most notable work was for the *Duck and Cover* satire film played in Hogarth's school as a musical animation about protecting yourself from an atom bomb. One particular sequence he storyboarded, where Hogarth's mother Annie goes on a date with Dean, was just too crazy to make it into the movie. The date featured Dean speeding through traffic, ordering a huge hunk of raw meat, bringing the meat back to his junkyard, slicing it with a jigsaw, cooking it with a blowtorch and serving it to Annie for dinner. Brad Bird thought Teddy's work was incredible even if he didn't fully understand him which led to Teddy being referred to as the X factor.

The Iron Giant has become a bit of a cult classic in that it wasn't a hit at the box office and didn't really become as well-regarded until its home video release. The problem was that nobody really knew how to market a film like this. When *The Iron Giant* arrived on home video, the TV promos did not feature any footage from the film. It instead focused on kids imagining themselves as giants, jumping and skating around a city as towering individuals. It was clear from this ad that Warner Brothers had no clue and/or no cares about marketing such a picture. But as time progressed and Brad Bird became a bigger name after he directed *The Incredibles* (2004), the film has slowly grown more recognized as the classic it should be.

The film was given a theatrical re-release in 2015 with new animated scenes based off original storyboards. One astonishing scene animated for this cut was the dream of the giant. While asleep, memories begin to surface of his life on other planets while serving in an army of killer robots. Brad Bird loved how abstract and intriguing this sequence was in storyboards, believing that the original theatrical release would have been just a little bit better with this addition.

The Iron Giant has an undeniable charm in how it presents a rather sweet and telling tale of a boy and his robot. With a striking parallel, many critics have compared its timeless sense of childhood adventure to that of *E.T.: The Extra-Terrestrial*. In response to the comparison, Brad Bird brilliantly stated, "E.T. doesn't go kicking ass."

THE LITTLE MERMAID

At a time when animated features seemed to be floundering, it was *The Little Mermaid* (1989) that was responsible for bringing about the second wave of successful Disney animations referred to as the Disney Renaissance. Some would argue it was *Who Framed Roger Rabbit* (1988) that started the Disney Renaissance, but that was too expensive and exhausting of a template to repeat. Prior to the release of both *Mermaid* and *Roger Rabbit,* there had been a great loss of creative juice at the studio ever since the death of Walt Disney in 1966. The studio was especially in trouble when animator Don Bluth left Disney to form his own studio. Not only did he take a handful of animators with him, but his animated features would be going head-to-head with Disney's. The studio desperately needed to reaffirm their standing as the dominant force in the industry before they would be kicked off the throne by one of their own. *The Little Mermaid* safely secured their title.

The key to their new success was infusing a new musical format with a hefty dose of Broadway. Howard Ashman and Alan Menken helped write the film's memorable melodies that burst from the screen with energetic and moving tones. "Under The Sea" was a bouncy Jamaican vibe in which the crab servant Sebastian (Samuel E. Wright) attempts to convey just how much fun it is to live in the sea. Clams are played as drums and coral reefs double as horns. The dancing of sea life and utilization of the surrounding elements for making music is absurd, but you can't help but fall for the catchy melody. So irresistible was this song that it was nominated for the Academy Award for Best Song.

Not to be outdone by the one song, the rest of the soundtrack was also nominated for Best Score. One of the most important songs from the film, "Part of Your World", was nearly cut from the film after it tested poorly with a child audience. Apparently, one child became more invested in cleaning their spilt popcorn than listening to this sequence. Thank goodness that data was ignored and the song remains. It's not so much because it garnered another award nomination, but because it's one of the pivotal emotional scenes in the picture and the most iconic with Ariel's angelic voice over a large splash of water against the rocks. When referring back to this film either for promos or from memory, this is one of the key moments that come to mind.

The character of Ariel marked a noticeable change in the Disney princess formula. She was independent, energetic and rebellious. Her red hair could symbolize power, but this design choice was mostly to separate her from Daryl Hannah's blonde mermaid character in the recent movie *Splash*. Not content to wait around for her prince, Ariel makes a deal to become human. She is aware of the risks and takes a gamble at a chance for true love above water. Her consequences are less severe in that she'll merely return to being a mermaid as opposed to the original novel where she transforms into seafoam. I suppose it'd be too tough for the Disney animators to make seafoam cute and bust out a tune.

Ariel makes the mermaid-to-human negotiation with Ursula, a sea witch with octopus tentacles. Designed several times as different animals (a scorpion fish among them) and inspired by many different actors (Joan Collins, Divine), Ursula was an unusually charismatic villain. Whereas previous Disney villains seemed to sneer and grovel in the darkness, Ursula was a delightfully jovial antagonist that was devilishly smart in getting what she wanted. She could also sing one heck of a fun song about dirty deals. Ursula grants Aerial her limited humanity, but only at the cost of her voice. Ursula then does everything in her power to prevent Ariel from kissing Prince Eric, including assuming human form and using Ariel's voice to woo the prince away.

Ariel's father, King Triton, feels just as realized as his daughter. He could have easily just been the cold figure that forbids Aerial from fantasizing with the human world, but Triton is given a surprising amount of fatherly anguish. He's tough on his daughter about visiting the surface, but worries about whether he's parenting correctly. You feel for him, but also find him frighteningly domineering. When Triton violently destroys Ariel's treasures to punish his rebellious daughter, it's terrifying with his glowing trident zapping objects in the darkness. But after he breaks her heart with destruction, there's a slight moment when his aggravated expression turns to sadness as he leaves her crying. That's a surprising amount of dimension for a parent that is placed as an obstacle for our heroine.

There's a little bit of charisma put into just about everything with this picture. Ariel brings her undersea treasures to Scuttle, a seagull that acts as a misguided expert on human treasure. Scuttle examines a fork and identifies it as a "dinglehopper" that is used for styling hair. Triton relies on Sebastian, a nervous and over-reactive adviser crab, to keep tabs on his daughter and aid her in the quest for love. Ariel's best friend Flounder, an innocent and childlike tropical fish, has a handful of cute moments. Even a ridiculously exaggerated French chef that tries to serve Sebastian for dinner has enough character for a silly song and slapstick sequence.

Watching the film as an adult left me in much more amazement at the detail of many of the underwater scenes. What specifically caught my eye were the bubbles. Watch closely as characters swim around the water generating dozens of bubbles. Someone had to draw all of those individual bubbles by hand - each of a different size, shape and direction. These details are especially worth noting as this was the last Disney animated film to feature traditional 2D animation. Future 2D productions would rely much more on digital technology for coloring and using computer graphics to fill out deeper environments.

The character animation is as vibrant and colorful as the best of Disney's features. Ariel bobs and weaves through the underwater kingdom with such enthusiasm for discovering the forbidden world of the surface. Her long red hair floats and moves freely in her aquatic environment. In the bright spots of the sea, her bright red hair compliments her deep green fins. In the shadowy interior of a sunken ship, the darker shade of red still looks beautiful. No matter the lighting, whether it was a morning sunrise on the beach or the evening skies at sea, underwater or above it, these characters look fantastic from every angle.

Having treasured the VHS copy for much of my childhood, I never noticed the phallic castle in the background of the cover that caused a bit of controversy. As with most Disney mistakes that are acknowledged as accidents, the penis-resembling structure was removed from future video covers. I did, however, catch the other visual controversy of the clergymen with an erection. Upon closer inspection, it was debunked as being his scrawny knees poking out from the clothing.

Disney chairman Jeffrey Katzenberg thought the movie was great, but initially told the staff during production that it wouldn't do as well as Disney's *Oliver and Company* because it was a movie for girls. *The Little Mermaid* grossed $84 million domestic on its first theatrical release, toppling that of *Oliver and Company* which made $53 million. Even when both films were re-released theatrically during the 1990's, *The Little Mermaid* still made more money, leading to a lifetime box office of over $200 million.

No matter the gender or age, *The Little Mermaid* remains a classic animated film that is visually stunning, musically charming and intelligently written. It also managed to prove that fairytales and musicals were no longer a dead breed of cinema. As far as the Disney studio was concerned, they were just getting started.

METROPOLIS

Though sharing the same title and themes as Fritz Lang's silent sci-fi classic, the Japanese animated film *Metropolis* (2001) was originally conceived as a comic book in 1949 (inspired by images of Lang's film). The comic book was one of the first major works by Osamu Tezuka, legendarily known for his contributions to Japanese art and animation. He worked tirelessly on a legacy of comic books, animated series, animated shorts and feature films. Though stricken with stomach cancer and confined to his hospital bed in 1989, he continued to produce right up until his demise. His last words were pleas to continue his work.

Since he departed this world, Tezuka's various works have lived on in the form of new animated series and movies based off his creations. The most grand and touching of all these tributes would have to be the theatrical adaptation of *Metropolis*. While the film doesn't quite have the same zip of comedy and drama Tezuka's stories were known for, director Rintaro does a wonderful job at capturing the overall spirit of Tezuka's comic book.

Rintaro was a fine choice for a director given his faithfulness to the style of comic book artists. He matched the cartoonish qualities of Leiji Matsumoto with *Galaxy Express 999* (1979) and maintained the detailed style of CLAMP with *X* (1996). He was also no stranger to working with Tezuka either as he helped with adapting *Astro Boy* into an animated television series. Rintaro had even pitched to Tezuka at one point about turning his *Metropolis* comic book into a theatrical feature, but was turned down at the time. It wasn't until years after Tezuka's death that Rintaro and Katsuhiro Otomo (*AKIRA*) decided to approach the prospect of the *Metropolis* film they wanted to make while still remaining faithful to Tezuka's comic book.

With *Metropolis*, Rintaro maintains Tezuka's style with all the big noses, rounded fingers and large eyes. He even brings a classic vibe to the picture's soundtrack by giving it a flavor of 1920's era swing and jazz. But he also alters the story more to appear closer to that of Fritz Lang's original silent film. There's a caste system in how the elite dominate the towering skyscrapers while the poor dwell underground in the mechanical innards that power the city. There's a robot built to resemble a human girl that could bring revolution, but also the apocalypse. Similar uses of the camera are also employed the way the screen will darken to a spotlight to bring our attention to something important in a scene. There's even a dash of *Doctor Strangelove* in how Ray Charles' "I Can't Stop Loving You" punctuates the apocalyptic climax of the film.

It's a film that wastes no time in showcasing the futuristic eye-candy. We see Metropolis' creator and ruler, Duke Red, stand atop his towering Ziggurat, a building that is secretly a giant weapon. The camera then sweeps and zooms around the tower from many angles as fireworks fill the sky and scores of people litter the street in awe. We soon learn this is a society where robots are used for menial labor that has phased out lesser human workers. Just as the poor humans are regulated to the underground, robots are given strict boundaries within the city as well. If a robot is found outside his zone, he is mercilessly gunned down by the Marduk Party, a militia organized to keep robots in their place.

Detective Shunsaku Ban and his nephew Kenichi visit the towering city on business to arrest Doctor Laughton on charges of organ trafficking. They wander around the busy streets of Metropolis in amazement, guided by a robot detective they dub as Pero. When Pero leads them down to the seedy depths of Metropolis' dangerous underground, they find Doctor Laughton's lab aflame with a girl inside.

When the fire displaces Kenichi from his uncle, he ends up further underground with the girl that goes by the name Tima. Similar to Maria from Lang's *Metropolis*, Tima is a robot born as a form of resurrection, resembling Duke Red's dead daughter, ultimately used for a sinister purpose. But Tima is kept innocently unaware of being a robot and is generally sweet. She slowly learns from Kenichi and grows to love him. Their friendship is mostly put on hold as a political coup and revolution breaks out across Metropolis.

For most of the picture, Kenichi and Tima are on the run. Rock, the adopted son of Duke Red, is aggressively pursuing them to kill Tima and regain the love of his cold father. Duke Red desperately wants Tima back in his care to have both his daughter and the instrument of true power. Tima wants to be with Kenichi, pining for his innocent lessons whenever she is torn from him. Detective Ban just wants his nephew back and maybe swipe some ice cream between the investigations. It's a solidly written story with plenty of tension, politics, pathos and destruction.

There are some rather sweet and charming moments throughout to prevent things from becoming too serious. When a fire breaks out at Doctor Laughton's lab, a clunky squad of firefighting robots is assembled to put out the blaze. Once they've wheeled and wobbled their way to the scene, a swarm of smaller robots form a protective shield around them while a hose-shaped robot pumps in water for the robots to use on the fire. It's a ridiculously over-the-top use of technology to fight fires, but it comes as a playful moment with the bouncy jazz soundtrack when the film seems to be getting a just a hair too serious.

One Tezuka trait that Rintaro preserves is the duplication/cameo of character designs. Ban is based off a commonly drawn character in Tezuka's work that is often referred to as Old Man Mustache with his walrus-like facial hair. Pero was the name of a robot character from Tezuka's *Astro Boy*. Many of the political and science advisors resemble several familiar Tezuka characters. Rintaro could have easily redesigned all of these characters to be more modern, but he remained true to Tezuka's trademark.

Rintaro presents a grand sense of vertical scale and depth to the towering city of Metropolis. When I originally saw this picture within the theater, not an inch of the screen felt unused. Most of the city is seen through wide shots where there is a multitude of details from robots of specific purpose to crowds ambling around the street. Take the scene where Duke Red walks the shady streets of Metropolis' lower levels as an example. On lower right of the foreground, two men greet each other and have a conversation. To the left in the shot, further in the background, two people kick a downed robot until it eventually explodes. When I viewed the film again on home video on my 19-inch screen, I could barely make out any of the small details in the background and foreground. It's a picture that begs for large presentations in both reading its actions and appreciating its detail.

Though the tone is quite classical with Tezuka's cartoony designs and that old jazz score, the animation was exceptionally modern. *Metropolis* came at an amazing time for animation where hand-drawn art and computer graphics complemented one another. In the case of *Metropolis*, traditional cel art was used for the characters while the backgrounds were computer generated. Such a merger of mediums could have been jarring, but it's a remarkable achievement in how well it meshes together. The throne room where Tima begins her rampage on humanity is brilliantly conceived with computer graphics as a metallic tomb where the walls glow and the floor comes apart. The characters perfectly occupy this space where they struggle to escape as Tima coldly sits on the throne with her clothes ruffling from the exhaust.

While *Metropolis'* script isn't terribly original with its themes of man's relationship with machines, borrowing much heavier from Lang's film than Tezuka's comic book, the film has an undeniable thrill as an epic spectacle of animation. Rintaro's vision of a futuristic city is realized in every aspect. There's a treat for the eye in every shot where background characters are rarely static and traffic is never so orderly. It's a living, breathing location of animation with unforgettable imagery and a thrilling adventure tale that lets us see it all. There's such craftsmanship and artistry to this picture that it becomes easy enough to distance itself from the false claim of being a remake to Fritz Lang's classic.

MY NEIGHBOR TOTORO

It's a little strange to believe that something as depressing as *Grave of the Fireflies* premiered as a double bill next to the heartwarming *My Neighbor Totoro* (1988). Both were Japanese animated films about kids trying to adjust in new settings, but they were vastly different in tone. While *Grave* was a testament to the hardships of children during war, *Totoro* was a celebration of the magic in childhood imagination. In its own weird way, such a pairing of films work if you chase *Grave of the Fireflies'* tears with *My Neighbor Totoro*'s smiles. Though, let's be honest, there's only one movie of the pair that parents would be okay with watching alongside their kids. Hint: it's the movie where the on-screen children don't suffer a slow death.

My Neighbor Totoro is all innocent and pure fun throughout. There is no earth-shattering conflict, no central villain to fight and no special mystery to unravel. There is drama, but it's never overplayed. There is a family-friendly charm, but it's never dumbed down. It's without a doubt one of the most playful and sweet animated films that came as a breath of fresh air in a medium where family entertainment appears far too frantic. *Totoro* slows down just enough for the audience to take in its beauty and magic, but never wanders too long in its own serendipity.

Two girls, Satsuki and Mei, are moving out to an old country house with their dad while their mother is in the hospital. It can be a downer to move away, but the girls are more than excited to travel somewhere new and different. They cozy up within the cramped car and share snacks with their dad driving up front. They're excited to be living somewhere new and are overjoyed at the sight of the dusty old house they'll occupy. As if they weren't already ecstatic, they discover little soot-ball spirits occupying the dirty old attic. And there are more mystical beings lurking about in the woods that the girls soon discover, none of which present any danger. Most of them are scrounging for acorns, taking a snooze in the woods or providing transportation. It's nice when spirits and mystical animals are not trying to drive you out of your home and welcome you to the neighborhood.

The titular creature exists as a giant, fluffy animal that constantly smiles and loves to help children. Though he towers over the two sisters that discover him, he's a gentle soul. Mei plops down on his belly. He gives a small roar at Mei and she roars right back. The two then curl up for a nap. Totoro later shuffles to a rainy bus stop with only a leaf on his head to protect him from falling droplets of water. Satsuki hands the giant beast her umbrella. Intrigued by the sounds of raindrops from the trees hitting the umbrella and not his head, the Totoro smiles excitedly and stomps on the ground to create a rainfall from treetop leafs.

The cuddly creature of Totoro became an icon of Studio Ghibli, appearing as the company mascot on their logo. He has become embedded in the pop culture landscape, cameoing in everything from *South Park* to *Toy Story 3*. The Totoro is a character that's become as recognizable and cherished as that of Winnie the Pooh or Mickey Mouse. Even if you've never seen the movie *My Neighbor Totoro*, the chances are high you've seen the character in some TV show or movie.

What's rather admirable about *Totoro* is how it plays on the perceptions of the older viewers. When the totoro first appears with his big toothy grin, there's uneasiness with many who view his smile as sinister and his size as dangerous. There's an immediate distrust with something so large and so happy. But that's all that Totoro really is. He's just a fluffy creature who wants to doze and frolic in the woods. The house the girls live in is old and creaky. There are several points where you expect the house to topple over into rubble, but it never does.

We hear that the mother is in the hospital and many will jump to the conclusion that she will die given the children's concerns. Despite the way films such as *Bambi* have conditioned audiences to believe that the parents have to die for the kids to have an adventure, mom never bites the dust. The thought that she might die is frightening enough for the two girls and the fact that she doesn't comes as a genuine relief. Mom and dad are gently pushed aside as either being at the office or in the hospital to let the girls have their own adventure. An elderly neighbor woman, referred to as Granny, provides emotional backup.

This is what makes *Totoro* such a great film not just for families, but for children in the way it plays on all their simple pleasures and fears. Kids like being scared, but not shocked to death by ghastly imagery. Something as simple as the wind rustling the house or dust mites in the attic are enough to put a little fright into the wee ones. At the same time, it also adds a thrill the way the girls delight in the discovery of spirits.

Relating to *Grave of the Fireflies*, the film does deal with death and how children think about it. A frustrated Satsuki uses the prospect of her mother's death to tell an over-reactive Mei why mom can't come home yet - Kei still whines and cries about wanting to her see her mother. When Satsuki is alone with Granny, she talks seriously about the prospect of her mother already being dead and breaks down into tears. Kids think about death in different ways and talk about it differently with other people. The subject is handled with a great deal of care in that kids will be able to relate to such feelings, but won't have to overly harp on them for the picture. Children still get to be children and enjoy their childhood in *Totoro*.

Similar to Miyazaki's other films, the little details that make *Totoro* shine. The way Mei follows her older sister around the house emulating her every action is both cute and telling of four-year-old girls. She has an admirable sense of determination the way she faces down soot spirits in the attic and sets off on her own to bring corn to her mother. Miyazaki is able to encapsulate the playful nature of children in a manner that doesn't feel artificial or one-note.

Though the story takes place in the town of Matsuko during 1955, the film has a timeless tone with its country setting. The children are surrounded by farming fields and woodlands with the nearest phone a few blocks away. The artwork by art director Kazuo Oga brings out a classic painterly style to the backgrounds, but doesn't date the picture in the least. I didn't even realize the era of the story was 1950's until I looked it up several years after my first viewing. It just goes to show how well Oga's work can evoke more of an emotional response than an eye for the decade.

Perhaps what makes *Totoro* so relatable is that its story is semi-autobiographical. Hayao Miyazaki's mother spent nine years in the hospital with spinal tuberculosis when he was only a boy. To not make the relation too obvious or too close to home, Miyazaki split the protagonists in two, changed their gender and modeled Mei after his niece.

My Neighbor Totoro was the second Studio Ghibli film to be released in America after the horrendous American cut of *Nausicaä of the Valley of the Wind* (1984) that was retitled as *Warriors of the Wind*. Angered over the butchering of his work, Miyazaki began his first instance of enforcing no editing on foreign releases of his films. This meant that names could not be changed and that not a single scene could be omitted for the American release in 1993. The result was a mostly faithful English release that was later improved with an all-star cast when Disney re-released the film in 2006.

The keyword with *My Neighbor Totoro* is heart. Hayao Miyazaki always manages to put some humanity in every animated film he directs, but *Totoro* is a special case where the warmth and charm is overflowing. He finds humor and drama in its most natural and tender of forms for two little girls. It's rare that a film can be so wholesome and honest for kids without the frenetic bells and whistles of most animated movies. That sense of realism amid all the fantasy creatures and simple joys of childhood is what makes it one of Miyazaki's universal classics for all ages. It's a cozy little picture that is always welcoming with a furry hug and a big grin.

PERFECT BLUE

There are times when I often wonder what some of the best directors in the history of filmmaking would craft in the realm of animation. Alfred Hitchcock was a master at using the camera to create eye-catching visuals and shots that seemed otherworldly. Imagine how capable his talents would be in animation which allows for limitless potential to lead and tantalize the viewer. Thank goodness there were directors like Satoshi Kon who knew how to use the medium to challenge and tease the eye more than just present it with colorful visuals. Roger Corman was quick to point out the comparison of Kon to Hitchcock and it's hard to argue against.

Perfect Blue (1997) is one of Kon's best animated features in that its script could be filmed in live-action, but wouldn't pack the same creepy punch seen through animation. There are certain shots in the film that use just the right angle, color and shadow to create an unnerving thriller that gets under your skin like no other animated film. Just the slightest tweak of the lighting, positioning of the camera and composition of the characters creates that uneasy tone of a haunting nightmare.

Mima is a pop singer turned actress after leaving her popular Japanese singing group CHAM. She's adored by her legions of fanboys for her angelic voice and bright frilly dresses that their hearts are broken by her decision to pursue an acting career. She's built up quite a devotion of fans over the years that will not stand for her new path. Stalkers begin to show their fangs in the form of a fan website called Mima's Room. The site contains blog entries of Mima's life that are not written by her, but matches the exact details of her day. Taking place in the early days of the internet in which Mima's first experience is this invasion of privacy is incredibly disturbing. The capper of a fax being sent to her with the words "traitor" written all over the message places Mima in a helpless scenario of being a constant target. She is losing control of her own life.

Further complicating her grip on identity is her latest project as an actress on the horror/thriller Double Blind. Mima stars as a rape victim and eventually the suspect of a series of murders that parallel her real life. Someone is brutally murdering all those responsible for Mima's new path. A staff member on Double Blind has his eyes cut out in an elevator for writing Mima into the show. A nude photographer is viciously stabbed to death for publishing erotic poses of Mima. Somebody wants the old Mima back and is willing to wipe out everyone responsible for taking away that pop singer figure.

Kon plays with the mystery more through the visuals and never wastes a moment of animation to wrap the story in twists of psychological horror. The overlapping of Mima's acting career and her actual reality begin to blur and blend. As the story progresses, there are several moments where both Mima and the viewer find themselves asking if what they're currently witnessing is part of the Double Blind program or if it is Mima's real life. She begins to see strange visions of her former pop star iconography, taunting her as a ghost from the past. With her angelic aura and condescending words behind that bright smile, the pop star in Mima tries to convince her that she has made a mistake and that those people had to die. It leads to more questioning if Mima herself is committing these crimes.

One problem with mystery movies is that once you solve the case, there isn't much left to go back for since you already know the ending. But *Perfect Blue* leaves plenty to analyze long after the mystery is revealed. Throughout the picture, Mima continually has visions of her pop star personality talking down to her in a perky inflection. Giggling and laughing at her failures, the glowing image appears everywhere and skips through the air. Is this Mima's split personality or her internal visualization of the vengeful id?

When the photographer is murdered in his apartment, we can visually see that the killer stabbing him looks like Mima. She plunges her knife repeatedly into the torso, each thrust flashing images of Mima's nude photographs at the screen. The scene ends with Mima waking up, suggesting that the previous scene was a nightmare. But she soon discovers that the photographer was murdered in the same manner she envisioned. The viewer is in a constant state of asking what is real and what is inside Mima's head.

The glowing spirit of Mima appears to one other individual: an overly obsessed fan referred to only as Mimania. To him, the imaginary figure he can see is the true spirit of Mima who has evolved past her physical form. In Mimania's mind, he hears the girlish voice of Mima begging him to right the wrongs of her name. By all accounts, this would be our primary killer. He's tall with dirty hair, protruding teeth and acts as a complete mute. We see his first appearance at Mima's farewell concert and then make the immediate connection after the first threat to her online privacy. But there is far more at play than the base assumptions from such a thriller.

The real danger isn't so much the killer as the icon of Mima. The new world that Mima ventures into is a long way from her simple days of puffy-skirted pop. She cites in interviews that she wants to be taken more seriously as an actress, but is this really what she wants? While acting on set, she plays a dancer that is raped on stage. Just before the rape begins, a cut is called and Mima freezes with a man on top of her while the crew readies themselves for the next shot. There's awkward silence between the two of them before being broken by the male actor apologizing. Mima brushes it off with cheerful acknowledgement that it's part of the job, but only after she lies there emotionless during the silence. The doubt is ever present as much as the pop idol character in her visions. This is a key scene as everything after this event becomes distorted from Mima's perspective.

Based on a novel, *Perfect Blue* was originally going to be a live-action film that was halted due to the 1995 earthquake in Japan. Though the live-action film did see the light of day in 2002, Kon's animated adaptation was far more engrossing as well as divergent from its source material. As his directorial debut, Satoshi Kon's career soon flourished as he became the director of such remarkable animated films as *Millennium Actress* (2001) and *Tokyo Godfathers* (2003).

The film originally had a tiny budget and was initially going to be a direct-to-video release in Japan. Due to its exceptional filmmaking, however, it was highly regarded as more of a theatrical film internationally. The result of its small budget is astonishing in how Kon economizes the right amount of detail to favor color and shots over intricately designed characters. Animated during the seemingly final years of traditional cel animation, there's a certain vibe and tone Kon achieves through this method. The camera work with exposures and subtle textures over the drawings have a dreamlike quality to them. The animation perfectly reflects the psychologically challenging state of Mima's world.

Perfect Blue is the type of animated film that stands firm as an example of how the medium is not just for kids. The film is a challenging mystery sufficiently grounded in reality, but evocatively presented through the lens of animation. It's an off-putting psycho-thriller that marks a refreshing change of pace from a medium that usually subscribes to comedy or fantasy. Animation is capable of delivering on any genre. Satoshi Kon knew it, animation buffs knew it and those who saw *Perfect Blue* would most likely agree.

PERSEPOLIS

As the technology for animation became easier and cheaper to use at the dawn of the 21st century, independent animated films opened the doors for all sorts of genres to be expressed through the medium. Animated films could now be made to cover any subject with any tone. Richard Linklater used digital rotoscope animation to conceive wild visuals for the talking heads of his philosophical drama *Waking Life* (2001) and for the trippy effects of his sci-fi drama *A Scanner Darkly* (2006). Nina Paley became a one-woman-army when she produced her animated film *Sita Sings the Blues* (2008) almost entirely on her own using computer animation software.

Persepolis (2007) opened another door for a different sort of animated feature that could be uniquely biographical. For being based on true events, the question arises of why it should be adapted into animation as opposed to live-action. While I'm sure the story could still be engaging in live-action, animation does a better job at encapsulating the life of Marjane Satrapi. We're not shown so much of Iran as much as Marjane's world that takes place in Iran. Marjane admits in the DVD commentary that the illustrated medium was intentional to make her story appear not so foreign to foreigners. It may not have been as effective considering a common American stereotype of foreign films is that they're in black and white (especially French foreign films), but it still creates a relatable nature with its clean and contrasting style.

Based on Marjane Satrapi's autobiographical graphic novels of the same title, the story follows Marjane's life in Iran from childhood to adulthood. Set against the Iranian revolution, the young Marjane is more interested in Bruce Lee and being a leader than recognizing the horrors of rebellion and war. Her parents are left-wing intellectuals and her grandmother was a rebel. She's aware of the current political climate with the Iranian Revolution, but only views it as seriously as a precocious little girl would. She smiles and boasts about her uncle spending more time in jail as a revolutionary than her friend's dad. Always asking questions and always playful, she has a universal childhood spirit that is slowly chipped away by the events that transpire from the rule of the Shah to Islamic Fundamentalists.

Marjane's rebellious heart pushes on through her teen years. As a teacher prattles on about political history, she finds herself more interested in talking with her classmates about western music. She visits a street dealer to secretly purchase an Iron Maiden cassette and rocks out in her bedroom with a tennis racquet as her guitar. She appears as a typically normal teenager in her personality, interests and humor. And normalcy is exactly what her family wants during an oppressive time where nearly everything western is banned. But you can only rock out in your room and bootleg wine for parties for so long before the oppressive regime creates a boiling point. Marjane, with her stubborn nature and questioning attitude, will not stand silent.

Having spoken up in school, Marjane is sent to Vienna alone for her own safety. Her enthusiasm for being able to shop for anything, sleep with anybody and say whatever she wants comes with a hefty price of her heritage. She is trapped between worlds: one where she is seen as an outsider and one where she is denied her individuality. Marjane slips in and out of depression, desperately trying to be an Iranian woman with the freedom to be her true self.

There is a genuine appeal in how *Persepolis* approaches its drama and humor without being forced. Marjane portrays her life with an honest tone devoid of pity and easy sentimentality. There are moments when she has fury and passion that hits the right level of anger towards the challenging world around her. There are times when she doesn't know what to do and succumbs to bouts of depression that plunge her into hopelessness. And then there are the pleasing moments when Marjane is able to pull herself out of a hole and press on with her off-key tune of Survivor's "Eye of the Tiger".

In addition to making Marjane more human in her illustrated portrayal, her tale is uniquely female. She speaks openly about her desire to shave her legs and how frustrated she is with the government's strict dress code for women. She deals with the difficulties of falling in love and then swearing it off when one relationship ends with her turning a guy gay. She rages with fire at the

Iranian soldiers who complain about her promiscuous features, arguing that they should just stop looking at her ass. Her grandma sweetly tells her how she would place flowers in her bra to smell nice all day. It's rare to see an animated film that presents such a fully realized female character that embraces all the humor and darkness that comes with growing into a woman.

A great deal of the film is narrated by Marjane. She breezes through the key background events to keep the story moving with matching visuals to keep all the exposition interesting. In describing her house hopping days in Vienna, we get to see quick visuals of her character literally jumping from house to house as she briefly describes the people she lived with. Her narration covers a hefty chunk of the film which could be seen as a deterrent for telling more than showing, but Marjane's story is a long one with many intricacies that need to be boiled down. She gives the audience just the facts and lets the visuals take over for the more interesting aspects of her life.

The simplistic animation style allows for great use of contrast and establishing moods more easily. There's a hilarious scene where Marjane describes her overnight metamorphosis into womanhood where we see her eyes bulge, her feet protrude out of her shoes and her breasts inflate until she collapses on the floor. Another brilliant scene features a young Marjane being harassed by two older Iranian women who move and act like snakes with their black robes. These fine details make a great case for both the use of animation and the insistence of the black and white visuals.

I also admire the methods of animation chosen for the picture. An early test reel reveals a scene of Marjane playing basketball with too much squash and stretch applied to her movements. Another test for lighting displayed how the use of gray shadows did not suit the style. The directors ultimately decided on a style of bold characters that moved believably with minimal exaggeration. The movements of the characters are simple, but it's that simplicity that adds to the realism of Marjane's story. That being said, I did enjoy her imaginative sequences of speaking with God and remembering her ex-boyfriend as a booger-eating slob.

Naturally, for criticizing the Iran that Marjane grew up with, *Persepolis* came with international controversy. The Iran Farabi Foundation objected to the showing of the picture before it had even debuted at the 2007 Cannes Film Festival, though it would eventually screen in Tehran with its sexual content was edited out. The Bangkok International Film Festival dropped the film from their lineup after speaking with the Iranian embassy. Clerics of Lebanon attempted to ban the film for its offensiveness to Islam, but later removed the ban after an outcry from the local populace. There was even a protest from as far out as 2011 when the movie aired on Tunisian television which led to the station owner paying a hefty fine for "violating sacred values". It feels strange to be writing about an animated film that has caused such an international stir for its subject and themes, but it's also invigorating to see such a daring nature in animation.

It's common to perceive animated films as restricted to the means of family fantasy in the commercial landscape. *Persepolis* is a fantastic example of how the medium can be used for so much more. After *Persepolis* was released, a number of biographical animated films followed that included *Waltz with Bashir* (2008), *Tatsumi* (2011) and *The Wind Rises* (2013) - all of which were told with a similar level of adult sophistication, engrossing as any live-action film could display such stories. Animated films don't have to just be about musicals and talking animals - they can be about social issues, the coming of age and the bittersweet complexity of life with a closer tie to reality.

PINOCCHIO

While *Snow White and the Seven Dwarfs* propelled Walt Disney's idea for animated movies into the American culture, it was *Pinocchio* (1940) that solidified his studio's dedication to storytelling. While he was grappling with the story elements of *Bambi*, hoping for it to be the studio's second feature, Walt was eventually convinced to go ahead with *Pinocchio* since it would be an easier tale to translate to animation.

Based on the 1883 novel by Carlo Collodi, it's a tale of morality that was more fixed than that of the short story *Snow White* was built from. As the second feature film of the Walt Disney studio, it also set a standard for how the studio would tinker and retool classic stories to be more likable and charming for the audience. This may be considered the studio's most enduringly maddening trend/sin, but consider the unlikable nature of the titular character along with the far more awful experiences he faces from the original novel; it's a liberty I don't mind so much that they took.

The biggest change Walt made from the original novel was giving Pinocchio more of that sweet innocence he had with Snow White. Collodi's Pinocchio was a bad boy that required much harsher forms of punishment to learn his lessons of being a good little boy. The character was rewritten to be more sweet and well-meaning in a world of scoundrels that would challenge his morality.

When the character of Pinocchio was first being designed, the wooden aspect was maintained in that the living puppet boy would look and move the way a wooden puppet would. Walt hated these initial concepts and demanded redesigns. It wasn't until animator Milt Kahl finally threw out the obsession of a wooden character and just made Pinocchio move more like a human boy than a puppet. The result is a puppet that moves more like he's made of rubber, but still has enough range to walk, dance, emote and react without appearing awkward in animation.

A similar approach was also given to the character of Jiminy Cricket, the talking cricket who acts as Pinocchio's conscience. He looks almost nothing like a cricket with his oversized head, lack of ears and his proper mode of dress. Animation supervisor Ward Kimball joked that Jiminy was only a cricket in the sense that they called him one. This was another character rewritten from the novel in that the cricket was a minor character killed early on by Pinocchio, returning to him in the form of a ghost. He made the picture work as the comedic mascot that would provide Pinocchio with advice, but also deflate scenes that may grow too dark.

Yet with all these changes to make the movie more upbeat and moral, it still features perhaps one of the most traumatizing moments in all of early Disney productions. After ditching school to smoke cigars and play pool on Pleasure Island with other bad boys, Pinocchio starts noticing something strange. The boys begin slowly turning into donkeys. Ears extend, teeth grow and hands begin turning into hooves. The scene where were shown the boys-turned-donkeys herded into pens and crates as they cry out for their mothers is still very chilling. These kids are never saved or turned back into little boys - there is a consequence for breaking the rules. It is only with Pinocchio's reaction and desire to change for the better that he narrowly escapes Pleasure Island, but only after growing donkey ears and a tail.

Pinocchio comes in contact with several villains of varying degrees throughout the picture. Honest John, a sly and manipulative fox, hoodwinks Pinocchio onto paths of acting and carefree pleasure in an attempt to make easy money. Stromboli, a large and loud puppeteer, greedily enslaves the boy for his own act. The sinister Coachman lures bad little boys to Pleasures Island where he transforms them into donkeys to be sold for monetary gain. And then there's Monstro the Whale embodying the cruel and massive force of nature. All of them have a surprising amount of character in how they go about their evil deeds. Honest John takes advantage of Pinocchio's gullible nature by using basic trickery of the eye to convince him that he is ill and that Pleasure Island is the cure. Stromboli is a hothead of a money lover who freaks out when discovering a slug token in his profits, but then devilishly passes it off to Pinocchio as payment. The Coachman appears as the most evil if not for his cruel nature towards the kids then for his company of shadowy henchmen. And what's so amazing about Monstro's character? Well, just look at the size of him!

The animation techniques of the newly formed Walt Disney Studio had grown immensely from their work on *Snow White*, a success that instilled them with much confidence. Since Walt didn't have to worry about funds so much for his second feature, he became more concentrated on achieving animation perfection. There is a larger sense of depth and perspective as seen from the variety of shots. Characters don't just appear in flat shots, but rather from different angles and all over the screen. There are aerial shots where we see Pinocchio's town from up on high. We look down at Pinocchio on the floor and look up at him on a stage. And, easily the most vivid set piece of the feature, Pinocchio's encounter with the massive whale Monstro is exciting and detailed to hook the eyes. Just watch how flawlessly these animators approached the depiction of water as Monstro takes the ocean into his mouth and spouts it from his blowhole.

The multiplane camera had been a tool that created a sense of depth on *Snow White* and was pushed further with *Pinocchio*. The opening shot of the village in particular took twelve different levels of planes to shoot. Rather than just zooming straight into the shot as was the case with *Snow White*, the camera would pan across areas as it continued to delve deeper into the shot. It was an expensive process seeing as how the multiplane camera cost $30,000 for every minute of use.

Another useful aspect to the animation process was the use of character models. Three-dimensional models of the characters were assembled with clay and provided to the animators as a means of referencing a character from any angle. This department didn't just end at characters, however, as they also built models of Geppetto's clocks, Stromboli's gypsy wagon and the Coachman's carriage. These models turned out to be more useful than previously thought as was the case with the gypsy wagon. The model of the wagon was filmed in stop-motion with the footage being transferred to animation cels to be drawn over. The final result is a wagon that moves very convincingly as it wheels across a bumpy road.

As with *Snow White*, the technique of rotoscope was once again used, but this time with a different intent. Live-action footage was shot to be used merely as reference for animating characters and not as a strict figure outline. This allowed for more natural movement and exaggeration as opposed to the stiffness of directly tracing over live-action footage.

Though a technical marvel, *Pinocchio* never reached the same level of financial success as *Snow White*. The presence of World War II greatly damaged the film's domestic box office and led to a loss of over a million dollars. Thankfully, however, critics responded quite favorably to the film. The New York Times gave it five out of five stars and the iconic song "When You Wish Upon a Star" won an Academy Award for Best Song (in addition to winning an Academy Award for Best Music).

Pinocchio represented a major shift for the Disney Studio. It proved that Walt wasn't just a one-hit wonder in how he dared to push the medium to its apex. The story opened the door to more mature storytelling that could touch on aspects of temptation and morality amid magic and adventure. For these many reasons, *Pinocchio* is often considered Walt Disney's best animated picture and a masterpiece of the art form. My nose would grow if I said anything less.

PRINCESS MONONOKE

Every American who was into Japanese animation in the late 1990's has a story to tell about their trek to watch *Princess Mononoke* (1997). With a limited release by Miramax, most states only had one or two theaters showing the film, often too far away for many to venture. I wish I could say that I had a story as well given how fans were driving as far out as four hours just to see the film. I was, unfortunately, in such a close proximity to so many theaters as my excursion was only a half-hour drive to the cinema at the Mall of America. For what it may be worth, the parking lot was awful.

Princess Mononoke ended up being one of those films that blew me away in my youth. Exiting the theater on that cloudy afternoon left me dazed in amazement at what I just saw. My mind was somewhere else. I knew I'd have to go back into the theater to find it. For the rest of the weekend, I made it my mission to see this film at least two more times.

In Japan, *Mononoke* was one of the biggest successes at the box office, almost reaching the same level as James Cameron's *Titanic*. Miyazaki's next film, *Spirited Away* (2001), would eventually topple that amount. In the United States, however, it barely made a dime from its extremely limited theatrical engagement. It was originally supposed to have a wider release, but Miramax chairman Harvey Weinstein reduced the theater count to 150 after being soured by producer Toshio Suzuki's demands for no edits. Suzuki's response to Weinstein's initial demands for edits was to send him a katana with a message: "No cuts." It does seem rather odd that Miramax would reduce the release after spending so much money on an all-star English voice cast that included Billy Crudup, Claire Danes, Billy Bob Thornton and Minnie Driver.

The story takes place in the Muromachi era of Japan - the narrator refers to the time period as an age of gods and demons. The spirits of the forest embody themselves within oversized animals that are currently being infected by a curse. The first scene reveals a giant boar roaring in pain as a force of black gelatin-like worms overtake his body, transforming him into more of a demonic spider. Prince Ashitaka defends his village from the beast on his faithful sable antelope, armed with his trusty bow. While successful in slaying the beast, it leaves his arm scarred with the infection of a curse. Deemed incurable by the town elder, Ashitaka is forced to leave his village forever.

On his travels to seek a cure, he meets both sides of the environmental conflict between the humans and the forest. He runs across the squat swindler Jigo who is curious about Ashitaka outside of his valuable goods. He meets the cute little Kodamas of the forest - white ghosts with bobbling heads that shake as if something were rattling around in their craniums. And he witnesses a rare sight by catching a brief glimpse of the god of the forest, appearing as a stoic elk with otherworldly qualities.

Keeping with Miyazaki's continuous themes of strong women, Ashitaka happens upon the Tataraba village led by Lady Eboshi. This independent society separate from the central imperialist government, employs women with jobs that include working the foundry and guarding the gates. Ill lepers are tasked with the building of bigger and better weapons. Eboshi's ambitions are to expand her colony into the forest which results in the creation of more cursed beasts. Rage fills Ashitaka's heart as he struggles to hold back his cursed arm from taking revenge.

Ashitaka soon meets San, the forest's only human warrior. Raised by giant wolves, she is known as the monster princess ("mononoke hime" in Japanese). Ashitaka first meets her from afar at a river where she bloodies her face to remove a bullet from a wolf. He later crosses her path during her assault on the Tataraba village. After knocking her out during her battle with Lady Eboshi, Ashitaka returns San to the forest despite a deep wound he incurs during his exit. Bitterly grateful for saving her life, San calls upon the spirit of the forest to save Ashitaka. The two slowly form a romance as they try to find a means of ending the feud between nature and man.

Princess Mononoke is certainly one of Miyazaki's most action-oriented and violent animated films, featuring plenty of dark moments with blood and decapitation. In US theaters, the violence was such a shock that it actually generated laughs in the audience. Some of these gruesome moments seem almost intentional in their comicality. A warrior is about to slam a blade into a retreating villager, but Ashitaka fires an arrow that slices off both of the warrior's arms. The warrior stares at his severed limbs in astonishment for a moment before freaking out.

To inform the public that *Princess Mononoke* was a more adult production, a change of pace from the usually family-friendly Studio Ghibli, Japanese promos featured the more violent scenes from the film. The few American television ads also made a point to emphasize the action with the addition of driving music. It didn't exactly stop little kids from going to see the film at the first screening I attended, but at least Miramax knew what they were marketing.

The film was also quite controversial as Miyazaki's most bold stab at environmentalism. The cursed gods come forth as a byproduct of human greed with Lady Eboshi's desire to mine the mountains. But unlike other environmental films that go for the simplistic struggle of evil industrialists versus peaceful nature, Lady Eboshi is not seen simply as a destruction-loving antagonist. She has taken in lepers and prostitutes to build a community that doesn't function on the shaming and cursing of others. She believes her ideals justify her need to push back the forces of nature for her own people. This makes her a very complex villain, though she still delights in firing a gun at a god.

Miyazaki gives a personal touch to *Princess Mononoke* as he does with all his films. Not content to just sit back in the directing chair, he oversaw thousands of the individual animation cels being drawn and actually redrew a hefty chunk of that amount. Though the film does employ a few minutes of computer graphics, in addition to some digital paint, the majority of *Princess Mononoke* was animated the old-fashioned way with ink and paint on plastic cels.

The English language version contains minimal script edits. A few strictly Japanese terms are substituted here and there to be more understandable to an American audience. One major difference between the Japanese and English versions is the casting of the mother wolf Moro. In Japanese mythology, wolves traditionally have male voices. As such, male voice actor Akihiro Miwa was chosen for the Japanese casting of the character. For the English language version, Gillian Anderson was cast for the role of Moro. While the

Japanese did cast a male for the role, it's worth noting that Miwa was a female impersonator.

Though the English script was rather faithful to the original Japanese version, the majority of Japanese animation fans wanted to see the original Japanese language version. When they heard the DVD release would only feature the English language version, they threatened a boycott. And since *Princess Mononoke* didn't exactly make a splash at the box office, Miramax caved to the demands of their devoted demographic. The DVD was delayed from September to December of 2000 and would feature the original Japanese version with an English subtitle translation.

Joe Hisashi conducts the musical score, as he does for nearly every Studio Ghibli production, but this is one of his best scores without question. It is heavily emotional, epic, driving and adventurous with beautifully soft violins and pounding drums. I was so amazed by this score that it was one of the first soundtracks I ever bought promptly after the movie. I took the CD home, popped it in my stereo setup and just sat there actively listening. I didn't busy myself with some other activities while the music played. All I did was sit there staring at the current track number on the digital display, letting the immersive music wash over me for an hour. For about a month, it was the only CD I ever listened to from driving in the car to studying at home. As I write this, I'm listening to the same copy of the soundtrack I purchased over a decade ago and it still gives me goosebumps.

Hayao Miyazaki had originally intended for *Princess Mononoke* to be his final film, but changed his tune after the film became a major success. He continued to direct many more animated films throughout his career including the Oscar-winning *Spirited Away* and the more adult drama *The Wind Rises* (2013). But *Princess Mononoke* could have very well been his last film and I would have been absolutely fine with him leaving his legacy off on such a brilliant animation. For being Miyazaki's most adult and violent animated film, I am still amazed at how transiently whimsical it manages to be with its lush renderings and epic storytelling. It's challenging, moving, gorgeous and frightening as the most powerful of fairytales.

ROYAL SPACE FORCE: THE WINGS OF HONNEAMISE

"How was I supposed to say if it was for the better or the worse of mankind?"

These are the first words narrated by Shiro as his younger self. He climbs a snowy hill to witness a naval aircraft carrier prep jets for takeoff. Despite taking place on Earth, we can tell from the technology being used that the world of *Royal Space Force: Wings of Honneamise* (1987) is not an era of any country we know of on this planet.

Shiro states his dream of wanting to be a navy pilot, but never being able to pass all the educational requirements. When we next see him, he's passed out at a bar as an adult member of the Royal Space Force. Being the member of such an organization may sound as if it's a proud position, but it has one major drawback: nobody on this planet has ever been to space.

The Royal Space Force itself exists more or less as a government organization that sends up a rocket occasionally and then buries the dead from the failed launch. Every launch has resulted in explosive failure. The "soldiers" find themselves bored with their duties that seem to be pointless. Shiro sulks next to a fence with his pal during outdoor training, lamenting about wasting his life. He later meets up with his comrades at a local tavern after work for gambling and drinks. A passing couple snickers and laughs at Shiro's Space Force uniform he didn't have time to change out of. The rest of the group is embarrassed to be seen with him.

While stumbling through the vibrant nightlife of downtown, where everyone around him seems to be getting laid, Shiro runs across the religious fundamentalist Riquinni handing out flyers. There's a certain admiration he shares for her passion and devotion.

Here is a section of town where everyone seems to be having the time of their lives, divulging in vices which are openly shared, and Riquinni appears in protest for what she believes to be a noble cause separate from simple pleasures.

After meeting with her and hearing more about her thoughts on life, Shiro becomes inspired to take part in what most of the Royal Space Force considers a death sentence: volunteering as a pilot for the next shuttle launch. The overreaction of his comrades does not sway his pride for opening humanity's door to the stars. Thus begins Shiro's long road of training, development and consulting for what he believes will be the first successful manned rocket launch into outer space.

Whereas most science fiction tales tend to favor a cast of passionate youth, the characters of *Honneamise* are older individuals. If they are not over the hill, they're certainly close to the top. They are a mostly tired and odd lot of soldiers and engineers. When Shiro pays a visit to the elderly group of engineers assembling the shuttle, dubbed the Space Travel Society, they're a cantankerous bunch of men bound by crutches and wheelchairs. Shiro notes that you can hardly talk to these guys and yet their genius minds work night and day to create something wonderful.

The launching of the shuttle itself is the crowning achievement of the Royal Space Force and the film. Caught up in a current war during prep, the Royal Space Force must launch from a site that is just a few miles from a country border where a battle takes place. Gunfire and bullets erupts in the distance as the crew prepare for the final launch. Jets zoom through the clouds, shooting down one another as they crash into the ground and shake the walls of the underground monitoring station. Tanks trade explosives as they push through grassy plains and make their way across rivers. There's intensity to it all, but everything seems to stand still once the shuttle liftoffs.

The film has had some harsh criticism for one scene in which Shiro attempts to rape Riquinni. He intrudes on her changing clothes and proceeds to force her towards the ground with a cold stare. She screams and struggles to break free, but Shiro doesn't stop until she looks up at him with a helpless expression. He snaps back to reality over what he is doing and stops, but not soon enough when Riquinni knocks him out with a frying pan.

The next morning, Shiro tries to apologize for his actions, stating that he let his desires get the better of him. But it is Riquinni who insists that she must apologize for hurting Shiro. While Shiro realizes what he did was wrong and how despicable it was, Riquinni remains confident that Shiro is still a good person who has the best intentions. She hasn't given up on humanity and wants Shiro to be just as strong.

This defines Shiro's struggle with being dedicated to doing something monumental. It is not an easy path as it is littered with harsh critics, violent radicals, crushing cynics and unnerving corruption. He begins to take an interest in Riquinni's religious teachings as a guide for his faith in his quest for the stars. This is a man who wants to be both a better person and fulfill some meaning in his life.

In the early stages of their relationship, Shiro implores Riquinni to be a little more easygoing. He gripes that he thought she and God would have come to a compromise by now. This angers Riquinni because she does not want to settle for half a decent life of spiritual fulfillment. In that same sense, she doesn't want Shiro to settle for just being a mindless grunt. He needs to pour his heart and soul into this project and it won't be the least bit easy.

When Shiro finally makes it into space, his scripted speech is lost as he gazes down at the planet. Being the first man to see the world from this view, he is humbled by the enormity of it all and simply prays for humanity. While he delivers this speech over the world, the film cuts to the planet's many facets. A bar fight develops between two bitter individuals. A little girl sits on a hill looking up at the stars. As sunlight bathes his craft, Shiro witnesses both moments of his own life and the entire planet - from the fires of cavemen to the pitter-patter of his childhood steps. Whether he actually makes it back to Earth or not is irrelevant as he has finally found both his purpose in life and his own meaning for all existence.

Wings of Honneamise was the first feature film from the fruitful Japanese studio Gainax. It was first presented as a four-minute short film to Bandai Visual for production. Much of the staff who worked on this production were fairly young and spun off into more renowned works. In particular, special effects artist Hideaki Anno would later go on to direct the popular Japanese animated TV series *Neon Genesis Evangelion*.

The film also managed to land acclaimed music composer Ryuichi Sakamoto, who in the same year won a Grammy for his work on the soundtrack to *The Last Emperor*. His score is a strange and compelling mixture of synth and traditional orchestra. The montages feature driving and upbeat electronic sounds while quieter scenes in country fields feature soft piano and violin.

The animation budget was a staggering ¥8,000,000,000, a record for a Japanese animated film at the time. That money was put to good use with Gainax having proven what they can do on a limited amount of money from their short films. Given as much as they had from Bandai Visual, they created an original, realized and detailed world unlike any animated film out there.

Every shot reveals just a little bit of this intricate world and all its aspects. It's all very other-worldly, but still grounded in its own reality where it doesn't feel odd for the sake of being odd. Everything fulfills a purpose from the strange headgear required for taking photographs to the bulkiest of architecture.

One of the most memorable shots from the film is a scene where Shiro flees from a street sweeper driven by a radical terrorist pursuing him. Shiro hops over a gate and dashes around a corner as the sweeper skids into a wall and continues the chase. So beautifully animated was this shot that it was practically stolen for another animated film, *Venus Wars* (1989).

Unlike such Japanese animated classics as *AKIRA* or *Ghost in the Shell*, *The Wings of Honneamise* never gained as much popularity. Toshio Okada, the former president of Gainax, remarked that the film was too much like an art film to be a mainstream success. Though the film didn't make back its staggering budget, it deserves to be noted as an animated classic for its intricate levels of detail. Such insane craftsmanship makes every repeat viewing just as amazing as the first.

THE SECRET OF NIMH

My earliest childhood memories of *The Secret of NIMH* (1982) are from my grandparents' house. They always seemed to have the more sophisticated animated films on home video from *Fantasia* to the Japanese version of *The Little Mermaid*. But it was *NIMH* that I kept coming back to the most. It's easy enough to see why with its displays of mysticism, sword fights, sci-fi elements, frightening beasts and an advanced society of highly intelligent rats. Its story had simplicity, but carries much deeper themes of morality and spirituality for older audiences. All these factors contribute to make *NIMH* a rare treat of adventure that's intelligent and exciting for all ages.

The director was Don Bluth, an animator from the Disney studio who left in the late 1970's to form Don Bluth Productions with *NIMH* being his directorial debut. It was a lofty choice to adapt Robert C. O'Brien's novel *Mrs. Frisby and the Rats of NIMH* into an animated feature. It went against the grain of storytelling he was used to at Disney – it was more dark and spiritual than anything they had previously produced. Such divergence was exactly what Bluth needed to stand out from the crowd in the tough battlefield of theatrical animation.

The Secret of NIMH went against the grain of standard Disney pictures in more ways than one. The most blatant being that this was a story Disney had previously turned down in the 1970's. Bluth had attempted to get Disney interested in such a project, but the studio was dismissive. Animator Woolie Reitherman reasoned that the Disney studio shouldn't try to repeat their efforts since they were already working on the mouse-centric film *The Rescuers* (1977). Going further against the big house of mouse was the opportunity Bluth was offered to him by former Disney executive James L. Stewart, who left to be the head of Aurora Pictures. Stewart acquired the rights for *NIMH* and gave Bluth a budget.

An opportune moment to prove himself and showcase the creative animators he assembled, Bluth was given a budget of $5.7 million and a timeframe of 30 months to complete *NIMH*. This was a vastly smaller amount of both money and time than what was standard for Disney. The pressure was on, but Bluth and his small band of animators was able to pull off a stellar film that could go head to head with any Disney feature. Countless nights and hefty loans all contributed to make *NIMH* a quality film.

The sacrifice for quality was worth it as *NIMH* is never a bore to look at it. Even if I didn't pick up on some of the film's deeper subject matter as a child, my young eyes were glued to the screen with the lavish amount of detail. The characters always felt alive with personality, even during scenes with long stretches of dialogue. From the comedic element of the clumsy crow Jeremy to the bitter nature of Mr. Ages, not a single character feels underused or even miscast. I can't imagine anyone besides Dom DeLuise voicing such an amusing character as Jeremy with his great comic timing. Bluth would later cast DeLuise as the trickster of his other animated films.

The backgrounds were amazing as when Mrs. Brisby ventures into the royal world of rats with all its cobbled together structures that are buzzing with lights. There's a fantastic element to the way everything is staged. The scene where Mrs. Brisby visits the cave of The Great Owl is exciting with the interior littered with bones, cobwebs and spiders. The extra attention to detail in the environment caught my eyes more as an adult the way reflections appear soft on a polished floor or ripple when seen on the surface of water.

But, as with any great animated film, it's the interesting premise that serves as bedrock for the spectacle. Highly intelligent rats escape from a laboratory at the National Institute of Mental Health (NIMH) and formed their own secret society on a farm. They steal from the farmers to provide electricity and supplies for their collective. But with their vast intelligence, they realize this way cannot continue and they must move on to a new way of living. Mrs. Brisby is caught in the middle of this struggle as she begs for help in preventing the farmer from destroying her home housing her sick child. As the widower of Jonathan Brisby, a mouse that helped free the rats of the lab, her name carries much weight as the rats agree to both help her and divulge more of their history. From her involvement, she discovers a plot which could bring about the end of their society.

Much like the structure of the similarly dark *Watership Down* (1978), *The Secret of NIMH* establishes itself in the human world, but creates its own secret world within. These are not semi-intelligent rats that misunderstand the world of humans or their actions. They are smart enough to know what they're doing and realize that they must change their ways if they want to evolve past their scrounging nature. As the elder Nicodemus put it best, "We can no longer live as rats."

There are familiar elements of xenophobia in how the evil Jenner fears the progress of their society that he's willing to kill for his own agenda. There exist fantastical dangers of their world as with the plowing of the field (referred to as Moving Day) and the presence of the aptly named farmer's cat, Dragon. The entire society of rats feel fully realized from their methods of transportation to their sense of community.

As with most books adapted to the screen, there are liberties taken with the material. Some were from a legal perspective in that the novel character of Mrs. Frisby had to have her name changed to Mrs. Brisby on account of the name being too close to the brand of flying disc toys. This change actually happened while the picture was already in production and the name change was made to the already recorded voices with careful editing. The most prominent addition to the movie was the magic amulet of Mr. Brisby that was passed down to his wife. The amulet is never entirely defined as to what it is exactly - it has often been referred to as the movie's deus ex machina in how its magical powers save the day. Whatever you call it, symbolically or literally, the amulet adds a magical dose of mystery to the world *NIMH* and makes it all the more alluring.

Jerry Goldsmith provided the music as his first composition for an animated feature. Approaching this project similar to how he would score live-action films, Goldsmith's music was remarkably magical and grand for such a small animated feature. He sets the tone perfectly for something that looks and feels like a fantasy. Due to the film's short production schedule, however, he would have to write music for scenes that had yet to be finished. Despite this issue, the music turned out rather well, especially with the additions of Sally Stevens and Paul Williams providing vocals for the tenderly sweet "Flying Dreams". Don Bluth's collaboration with Goldsmith ultimately led to him meeting Steven Spielberg who would help Bluth produce *An American Tail* (1986) and his future animated films.

Released in 1982, *The Secret of NIMH* was a bit of a failure with little advertising and appearing in few theaters. It also had to compete in a crowded year of popular genre pictures that included *E.T.*, *Tron*, *Rocky III* and *Star Trek II: The Wrath of Kahn*. But it has proved the test of time as cable viewings and video sales brought up its popularity and made it more financially successful over time. The film also helped define Bluth's controversial style of direction that didn't fear darker aspects of storytelling. His later animated movies, *The Land Before Time* (1988) and *All Dogs Go To Heaven* (1989), did not shy away one bit from the subjects of death and redemption. Even his more bouncy musical *Rock-A-Doodle* (1992) was rather bleak.

But *The Secret of NIMH* remains one of Bluth's best for its balance of darkness, tenderness, heroism, mysticism and adventure. It has a style and tone that is equal parts classic and timeless for a fantasy picture in the grandest of traditions. At a time that was considered the dark ages of Disney animation, *NIMH* shines brightly as an example of quality filmmaking that was more than just another animated mouse movie.

SNOW WHITE AND THE SEVEN DWARFS

Snow White and the Seven Dwarfs (1937) wasn't just a primitive first step in the genesis of animated feature films. It was a massive leap in that it was revolutionary rather than just being an animated short padded out to over an hour. There were bold colors, vibrant movements, breakthrough camera techniques and heaps upon heaps of details in every shot. Animation was no longer just a short distraction to tag to the beginning of motion pictures.

To reach such status, Walt Disney had to push past many boundaries and find new techniques to amaze the audience on the same level as a live-action picture. There were plenty of voices against his ambitious project including his brother Roy Disney and wife Lillian. It was a massive undertaking with a budget of $250,000 that soon ballooned to over $1,400,000 - incredibly expensive for a studio that was only producing shorts. Walt Disney had to mortgage his house at one point to keep production going. He even had to screen what he had finished to convince a banker to provide more funds. There was a lot riding on this one film that seemed to be too big for its own good. Animation in the 1930's was strictly relegated to a series of shorts you'd watch before a film. The idea of blowing up the medium to a feature-length running time must've seemed absurd at the time. During its production, it was dubbed as "Disney's Folly".

But try to imagine the first viewing of *Snow White* during that era. When cartoons were simple distractions of rubber-hose creatures and silly gags, Walt took audiences into a colorful kingdom of beauty and wonder. Snow White enters the screen not as an exaggerated figure, but a fully articulated woman. The talking mask inside the magical mirror appears as an ethereal being of smoke and light. Charmingly silly dwarfs with varying personalities sing their way through a day of mining with a timelessly catchy tune. The audience is taken into a world of magic, fantasy, danger and joy that was never felt before with animation.

The idea to use the tale of *Snow White* for his first feature-length animation was an easy enough decision for Walt. It had sympathetic dwarfs, a sweet princess, a jealous queen and a romantic prince. To Walt, it was both basic and perfect. Disney's ultimate goal with *Snow White* was to bring more personality to animation and evoke more emotions than just simple smiles and gags. He wanted the audience to be scared as Snow White finds herself lost in the woods. He wanted us to feel sadness when she falls into a deep sleep as the dwarfs watch over her. One of the biggest moments of terror occurs when the Huntsman moves in on Snow White with his knife, preparing to slay her before eventually having a change of heart. During the numerous story meetings to discuss every detail of this scene, an animator asked, "Won't she get hurt?" There was a believability that had been built up through these discussions that made Snow White a real character that the crew cared about.

It's easy enough to look back at early films of the 20th century and balk at their acclaim. The biggest fault many cite for *Snow White and the Seven Dwarfs* is that the titular princess is a very boring character. They are not wrong. She is a character where more parts of the story happen to her rather than from her. The same goes for the prince who doesn't do much else either. That's why the film itself isn't so much about her or the prince. The secondary characters steal the show and half the title. They have the best songs, the funniest scenes and a wider range of character.

The dwarfs can embody the audience easier as was the case with Grumpy. He's a cynical character that provides the perfect contrast to the overly sweet nature of the film. His mocking and dissatisfaction in going along with anything in the story helps make the picture easier to swallow for those not in the mood. When first meeting Snow White, Grumpy wants her out of the house as he's familiar with the queen that is trying to kill her. He knows about her powers and believes that if his dwarf family harbors Snow White that they could be killed as well. Snow White simply says that the queen will never find her and changes the subject to why she should stay. All are swayed except for Grumpy. His bitterly cautious nature is more identifiable for those that don't want to buy into the fantasy of the film.

There were plenty of innovative techniques Walt Disney

employed on Snow White to make it stand out as a landmark of animation. He had previously used a tool called the multiplane camera on his animated short *The Old Mill* (1937) to create a deep sense of depth. Rather than shoot one flat painting in front of a camera, several layers of paintings were placed on top of each other and the camera slowly moved between them. This illusion of depth was used to greater effect in *Snow White* as you can see in the opening shots of the castle. The multiplane camera became an essential tool for the many Disney animated features that followed.

Snow White and the prince were animated with rotoscope, a technique where live-action is traced over by the animators. The drawings were then embellished and exaggerated to fit better into the animated setting. Such a technique may sound simple in that it essentially sounds as if it was little more than tracing, but rotoscoping humans turned out to be a real challenge for the animators. Drawing a fully formed human, even with a heaping supply of reference footage to work from, was not something the animation team was accustomed to drawing. For this reason, several of the shots with the prince were trimmed down as they just didn't look right when animated.

Essential to animating the character of Snow White was the addition of animator Myron "Grim" Natwick, known at the time for his work on the Betty Boop cartoons. Walt saw the way Natwick paid close attention to Betty's hair and dress reacting to changing forces. There was a feminine quality to Natwick's style of animation that Walt knew he needed for Snow White. You can see it present as when Snow White primps her hair or pulls her skirt along as she dances with the dwarfs.

Walt was very meticulous about trimming down the picture to perfection. Several scenes were animated, but never made the final cut, such as a song of the dwarfs eat soup and an extensive scene where the dwarfs build a bed for Snow White. Animator Ward Kimball's tireless work on the soup sequence was not a complete waste, however, as Walt made it up to him by giving him control of the Jiminy Cricket character in Disney's next animated feature, *Pinocchio* (1940).

Snow White and the Seven Dwarfs was a monumental hit for Walt Disney. It was so successful that over time Disney grew to hate the picture in how every film he made after was compared to *Snow White*.

When he previously made the animated short *Three Little Pigs* (1933), it was so successful that theater owners were eager to see a follow-up. Walt gave in and made more short segments about the pigs that were not as successful. "You can't top pigs with pigs," Walt Disney proclaimed. In that same sense, you can't top dwarfs with dwarfs, though there were certainly many who disapproved of *Pinocchio* because of that. While Disney's next batch of animated features didn't approach the same level of box office, they were no less of classics that have just as much perfection if not more.

The success of *Snow White* opened the gates for Disney's future. He used the profits to build his own studio in Burbank where his team of animators would complete more animated features in a surprisingly timely manner. The film won an honorary Academy Award and was nominated for the Oscar of Best Musical Score. Its success inspired the film industry to pursue more fantasy-based projects in both animation (*Gulliver's Travels*) and live-action (*The Wizard of Oz*).

In addressing the future of his company, Walt Disney remarked that his only hope was that everyone remembers that it was all started by a mouse. *Snow White and the Seven Dwarfs* deserves to be just as memorable for the creation and inspiration of animated features - it was all started with a princess, a queen, a prince, some dwarfs and an apple. And animated movies lived happily ever after.

SPIRITED AWAY

I first caught *Spirited Away* (2001) on its limited theatrical run at the Uptown Theater in Minneapolis. It wasn't my first time to the theater, but the first time I'd ever waited in a line that wrapped around the block. The theater was a packed house that sat in amazement at the awe-inspiring animation. Another first for myself was the standing ovation given upon the credit roll with every attendee standing up as if director Hayao Miyazaki himself was about to come up on stage. Keep in mind this was a Sunday afternoon showing.

What was it about Miyazaki's *Spirited Away* which made it such a beloved film of his career and the first of his to earn an Academy Award for Best Animated Feature? I would argue that this is one of the director's more accessible works for the mainstream. Most of Miyazaki's animated features tend to delve straight into the magic and fantasy of a different world, plopping the viewer right in the middle of its own wonder. *Spirited Away* approaches the mystical land of spirits with a very relatable child to keep things grounded.

Chihiro is a believable little girl, bummed by moving to a new town. Her parents are far too adventurous as they become distracted by the presence of an abandoned amusement park. The parents decide to explore the grassy area of old buildings while Chihiro begs them to go back to the car. She's either seen a few horror movies or heard a few ghost stories as all the signs of spooky movie logic point to getting out of there. The parents find some freshly cooked meat and dumplings at a desolate shop and proceed to partake of the offerings. "Don't eat that stuff!" shouts both Chihiro and the audience. The parents are quickly turned into mindless pigs so that we can get on with Chihiro's adventure.

As the sun sets, the desolate amusement park soon turns into a busy town of beautiful lights. All manner of creatures and beings appear before our frightened heroine. Talking frogs, giant birds, walking radishes and masked ghosts fill the streets. The only human-looking character on the street, Haku, prevents the girl from being discovered as a human, instructing her on how to get her parents back and go home. To do so, Chihiro must seek employment at the bathhouse, managed by Yubaba, the evil old witch with a ridiculously oversized head. But Chihiro must first ask for a job from the boiler-man, Kamaji, an old grump with spider-like arms that can multitask. Her journey proceeds with meeting one unique and colorful character after another in this fantastically magical world. As film critic Richard Roeper described it, "It's as if every child in Japan did a drawing and they put all these characters into a movie."

While there is certainly a lot of amazing moments of animation and design, the film still has time to stop and breathe. Hayao Miyazaki includes several quiet scenes that are referred to as "ma" to break up the action. There are scenes where not much seems to happen – Chihiro opens a window and observes the blue ocean surrounding the bathhouse. These scenes are not dull as there is plenty of gorgeous scenery and lots of little details to keep the eye pleased.

In constructing the character of Chihiro, Hayao Miyazaki wanted to strive for a very relatable element of an ordinary girl. He didn't want her to be overly pretty, but didn't want her to look too dull either. After much design, Chihiro resembles a girl that's the right mix of average and cute. Her adventure is also one that isn't atypical for ten-year-old kids. She's given plenty of challenges to face, but never has to do anything all that epic - there's no beast to slay, treasure to unearth or prophecy to fulfill. It's a story that relies on her wits and inner strength to find her way back home and become a more independent person.

As with many of Miyazaki's films, the bulk of the inspiration came from his own life and experiences. The character of Chihiro was inspired by his associate producer's ten-year-old daughter. Upon meeting this girl and her friends during a family vacation at his mountain cabin, he became intrigued by their apathetic mannerisms and attitudes. Devoted to making strong women in his works, Miyazaki believed he was missing out on a demographic. He had made animated films with appealing characters for children and teenagers, but not for tweens.

Miyazaki took a look at some of the romance comic books the girls were reading and didn't see much of the heart he admired about real girls. Having not seen the type of media that ten-year-old girls deserved, Miyazaki set about to give them a real heroine with *Spirited Away*. In doing so, he additionally gives the young people a kick in the pants by presenting them with a mythical tale that could be engaging on their level.

He inserted several old elements of Japanese culture that most modern Japanese children would not understand. There's a moment when Chihiro steps on a cursed slug, makes a triangle with her fingers and Kamaji has to break it for her. This is an action that is seen as a form of good luck or the Japanese equal of a cootie shot, but the young Japanese actress voicing Chihiro had no idea that's what it was. Miyazaki had to explain it to her during a recording session.

Before Miyazaki had the inspiration of a little girl, however, he still had an idea for the setting. His hometown bathhouse always appeared as a strange place to Miyazaki as a child, imagining what mysteries could lay beyond doors he never opened there. From that imaginative curiosity, he conceived stories about how a bathhouse might be run. He used this setting for two other story ideas he was developing before *Spirited Away*, but they were both rejected. Adding some more of his local experiences, the scene where Chihiro and the bathhouse employees remove a bicycle from a spirit's insides is based off the time he and others pulled a bike from the local river while cleaning it.

The animation, once again personally helmed by Miyazaki, mixes both the traditionally hand-drawn and the computer-aided. Though more computer animation was used than that of Miyazaki's previous film, *Princess Mononoke*, the animators were careful not to let the new technology overshadow the old techniques. Most of the computer animation compliments the dreamlike nature of the picture as when Chihiro is led by Haku through a tight wall of flowers. The hand-drawn animation, however, still remains the biggest draw of the film with its expressive characters, vibrant colors and great lighting. There's an immense level of detail with all the little elements such as the dirt on feet or the decay of old wooden buildings. In one of the most amusing shots where Chihiro's father heads toward the camera aimed at a low angle, you can briefly see the swaying zipper of his pants.

The tremendous amount of detail lends to Miyazaki's desire to create a believable world even when it's a fantasy. There's a scene where Haku transforms into a dragon-like creature and Chihiro must force-feed him medicine. Miyazaki described the creature's mouth akin to that of a dog. Since nobody on the animation team owned a dog, Miyazaki brought them to a veterinarian's office and filmed reference footage of a dog's mouth.

Given how much more grounded Miyazaki made *Spirited Away*, this may be the first time he's used rather blatant product placement to create a convincing modern reality. In the opening scene, Chihiro's family is driving in an Audi A4 Sedan. Though the car model is never stated, the insignia on the front of the car makes it very clear it's an Audi. The animators even took advantage of a scene to showcase the "Quattro" four-wheel drive and anti-lock brakes system as Chihiro's father recklessly drives up a hill.

Acquiring the rights for *Spirited Away* came with stipulations for both Ghibli and Disney. After having a bad experience in how Miramax handled *Princess Mononoke*, Studio Ghibli did not want any edits made to their movies. Disney agreed on the condition that they were allowed to have the rights to all of their movies. Thanks to this deal, future Studio Ghibli films would be given American theatrical releases while past Ghibli classics would receive proper American home video releases. These video releases were how many Americans would discover and enjoy the previous masterpieces of Studio Ghibli with a faithful English version produced.

Pixar's John Lasseter was chosen as the executive producer for the English version of the film after Disney acquired the rights and it couldn't have been a better choice. Lasseter adored the works of Miyazaki so much that he would often sit and watch his movies when encountering story problems with his staff. Lasseter was also no stranger to Miyazaki as he had previously visited Studio Ghibli to showcase his CGI shorts *Luxo Jr.* and *Red's Dream*. Despite having an initial distaste for computer animation, Miyazaki found the shorts rather charming.

Spirited Away became the first Japanese animated film to win the Academy Award for Best Animated Feature. Additionally, it was one of the longest movies to win at the time - clocking in at 125 minutes. And it would have been even longer if Miyazaki didn't trim down his plot which he believed would have made the film over three hours long.

The success of *Spirited Away* in box office and acclaim was no fluke. For years after it was released on home video, it has been the most requested DVD from my personal video library for entertaining kids. I've even lent my copy out to teenagers that wanted to borrow it. The movie seems to have this resonance of imaginative wonder, childhood adventure and pure fantasy that sticks with you longer after the first viewing. *Spirited Away* is Miyazaki's masterpiece and I'm pleased to see that it continues to be recognized as a timeless fairytale for all ages.

THE THIEF AND THE COBBLER

Animated films take an awfully long time to produce. Over the course of many years, everything can change from the style to the script. No animated film went through more internal problems than *The Thief and the Cobbler* (1995). The project was passed from editor to editor, producer to producer, voice actor to voice actor, animator to animator and distributor to distributor. It is known by many names for its various cuts including *The Princess and the Cobbler* and *Arabian Knights*. For the many edits and changes the film had undergone - from official to unofficial - it is considered by many to be the greatest animated film that was never truly finished.

This was a frustrating work of animation with origins that date as far back as 1964. Animator Richard Williams became inspired by the written works of Mulla Nasruddin after having illustrated for a novel collection by Idries Shah. Williams soon decided that he wanted to direct several films based on these tales. It became a project of passion, slowly fueled by his commercial work.

While Williams continued to tinker away at his project for many years, he was faced with several obstacles. There were negative roadblocks such as the bad accounting that led to disagreements about the film's development. There were positive roadblocks in that Williams was fortunate enough to be involved with the grand production of *Who Framed Roger Rabbit* (1988), which won two Oscars for his visual effects work. After years of working with several creative animators and interesting financial backers who soon backed out, Williams finally landed a fully funded production with Warner Brothers in the late 1980's.

But even more complications arose from working with Warner Brothers. Although Williams was able to add many new scenes and record some additional dialogue, a strict deadline for the film forced him to overwork himself and his animators. He fought tirelessly to achieve the perfection he desired and would often fire animators that were not delivering quality results in a timely manner. Despite Williams' cracking of the whip and working day and night, the film was still not completed by 1991. The rough cut he displayed in 1992 with a missing reel did not impress Warner Brothers, leading to them kicking him off the project and employing Fred Calvert to finish the film. Calvert originally didn't want to take on the picture, but decided to do so out of concern that a cheaper director might do worse.

Despite several changes, some of Williams' brilliant animation remained in the butchered versions released. The setting of Golden City is portrayed with flat geometrics and vibrant colors. It challenges the eye the way characters occupy such odd perspectives, appearing as though their walking on top of a painting. The hypnotic dimensions of the backgrounds bring more attention to the characters who establish distance and depth in their actions. It's worth noting that this animation was all hand-drawn, especially during many of the sweeping shots over the city that turn the camera and change perspective.

The characters themselves are uniquely designed with varying proportions. The plucky cobbler Tack is seen as a lanky man of baggy rags with a tack constantly in his mouth. The nameless thief appears as a moving blob; consuming any and all valuables under his large cloak (he even steals the credits by the end of the film). The evil Zigzag, a Grand Vizier to Golden City's king, has a very freeform shape that stretches and distorts with his sinister means of taking over Golden City. Richard Williams described Zigzag's movements as that of a marionette with extra joints. His arms and fingers can bend and distort at many different angles. If you look closely, you'll notice that Zigzag has six fingers covered in rings on each hand. The unnatural anatomy of Zigzag makes him an amazingly fun character to watch.

Though the design of the characters is fairly simplified, they're given an enormous amount of complexity when placed in animation. The scene where the thief balances himself across a long chain as though he were walking a tightrope is packed with perspective, weight, distance and character. The thief appears simple enough to animate and the background has been simplified to the color of the sky, but the commitment to adding such detail in one continuous shot is what makes it remarkable. It's one of the many strong displays of fluid character animation throughout the picture.

The voice cast on the project varied over the course of production. The one constant was Vincent Price as Zigzag. He played the villain so well with the right level of sinister inflection that you just couldn't replace him. Most peculiar about the various versions were the voices added to roles which originally had little to no dialogue. The protagonist of Tack only had one line in the original version which would have been spoken by Sean Connery if he had showed up at the studio. The one line was instead delivered by William's wife's friend who is uncredited. In future versions, Tack's voice was expanded in narration spoken by Steve Lively and eventually Matthew Broderick for the Miramax version.

The thief himself was never intended to talk at all in the original version, but later versions featured him talking his head off with internal dialogue. Jonathan Winters is not a bad choice when it comes to selecting voice talent, but you can spot him struggling hard to keep the voice of the thief going. Voicing many scenes of the silent thief, Winters' insertion plays more like outside commentary than an actual role.

Another altering element to the various versions was the presence of songs. Williams never intended the film to be a musical, but since Disney was laying claim over the industry in the 1990's, musical numbers in animated films seemed to almost be a requirement. Fred Calvert's 1993 version (*Arabian Knights*) deviated heavily from Williams' workprint and inserted four songs into the film. A few were cut for the Miramax release in 1995, but the musical aspect still remained.

Soon after Calvert's version was released, Williams' original workprint was bootlegged and circulated among many animators and animation fans. Walt Disney Feature Animation head Roy Disney took a look at this workprint in 2000 and decided to restore Williams' original vision with a restoration project. But when Roy left Disney in 2003, the project was eventually put on indefinite hold.

But the fans ultimately became more devoted and fruitful in preserving Williams' cut of the film. Garrett Gilchrist, a filmmaker and fan, created a non-profit initiative for a fan-edit of the workprint titled *The Thief and the Cobbler: The Recobbled Cut*. Supported by much of the original animation staff, the fan-edit combined finished and unfinished footage to make the workprint version more complete.

The Recobbled Cut has been revised and updated over the years as unearthed materials from the animators were donated to the project. It is widely considered to be one of the most intricate and elaborate fan-edits ever made.

Despite the overlong production and executive meddling, *The Thief and the Cobbler* is an animation masterpiece unlike any other (even if it's mostly respected in its workprint form). It's rather hard to recommend in the form of a fan-edit, but it's a version worth seeking out given the dreadful treatment by Miramax. In its workprint form, the film has become an inspiration to several animators and filmmakers, most notably director Tom Moore who directed the Oscar-nominated animated films *The Secret of Kells* (2009) and *Song of the Sea* (2014). The workprint version would also be archived by the Academy of Motion Picture Arts and Sciences. Such a picture deserves far more praise than the scoffing of being an *Aladdin* clone when the film was retooled to appear as such.

TOY STORY

In 1937, *Snow White and the Seven Dwarfs* became the first feature-length hand-drawn animation that was a massive achievement. In 1995, John Lasseter pioneered the first feature-length computer-animated film *Toy Story*, created by Pixar and produced by Disney. From that accomplishment, the Pixar studio became a household name and an entirely new form of animated film was born for the 21st century.

Computer animation could render a new and different world filled with limitless possibilities. Lasseter saw all that potential when he was mesmerized by Disney's first big attempt with the lightcycle sequence in *Tron* (1982). He loved the idea of using those effects to craft an entire animated universe that could exist independent of drawings and live-action. But Disney wasn't interested and kicked him out. It took Lasseter's award-winning CGI short *Tin Toy* to convince them to hire him back and accept a deal that would allow Pixar Studios to exist as its own studio for films that would be distributed by Disney.

After some negotiations, *Toy Story* began production, but this wasn't a solidified idea right out of the gate. Most of the hang-ups for *Toy Story* came not from the technical limitations, but the creation of the story itself. At first, it appeared closer as a continuance of *Tin Toy* with the one-man-band toy Tinny partnering up with a ventriloquist's dummy on an adventure. Their journey would eventually lead them to a preschool where they would never be discarded by their owners, a concept that would later be used for *Toy Story 3*. Disney chairman Jeffrey Katzenberg rejected the idea and told Lasseter to go for more of a buddy picture. Several drafts continued including some versions where Tinny was still the lead.

Eventually, the characters of Woody and Buzz Lightyear appeared in the script, but far from the polished final product. In the early versions, Woody was a jerk. He insulted the other characters and made bad jokes at their expense. It made him much harder to care for when he's torn from the room and must find his way back while learning a lesson. Thankfully, after many more drafts, Woody materialized into a more likable personality with a far greater character arc.

Pixar established their trademark technique in this film for building unique worlds. Seen from their perspective, the toys are sentient only when nobody is watching. They gather together in Andy's room after each play session to discuss upcoming events. Their long-term crisis involves Andy moving with his mother to another home, making the toys begin preparations for buddy systems when being packed.

The immediate crisis, however, arises when Andy's birthday party has been bumped up without their warning. They panic and cower around the window as guests arrive with presents. The toys look on with concern at the possibility of being ushered out of Andy's room for new and better toys ("Yes sir, we're next month's garage sale fodder for sure"). The toys soon take a liking to the new toy Buzz Lightyear, but Woody grows jealous as Buzz kicks Woody off the throne as Andy's favorite toy. Thus begins a buddy picture where the two must learn to work together when they are separated from Andy's room.

From the first shots of Andy's room, we establish a heavy scope of space and scale for these toys. Some toys are as large as dolls and some are as tiny as army men. Some are complete forms and others come in pieces. When Woody sends out a group of army men toys to run recon on the birthday party, they haul out a toy walkie-talkie which takes many of them to carry. They dive down the stairs with parachutes and stash the walkie-talkie in a potted plant to maintain communication with Andy's room. This scene establishes everything that is needed to create the believable and mesmerizing universe of *Toy Story*.

Aside from great camera work and character animation, the effects of the film made it stand out vastly from other computer animations of the time. Little touches such as the reflection inside Buzz Lightyear's plastic dome, the soft terrain of Andy's bed, the fingerprints on the door handles and the smudges of aged marker all give believability to this world. These effects were a combination of both technical innovation and real research. For a scene where Woody has his forehead burned by a magnifying glass, art director Ralph Eggleston actually burned a doll head to reference the right level of damage and color. Even the human characters, which would much be more difficult to create than inorganic toys, look and act believably from the waist down and up. They would have to be just as convincing as the toys considering how much time we spend with Sid, the nasty neighbor kid who delights in destroying toys.

There wasn't a lot of initial faith in Pixar working on something so ambitious, being both a CGI feature and a buddy picture. But in an animation test from 1992 in which early forms of Buzz and Woody converse in a fully rendered piece, most of these worries were put to rest. As the animation process progressed and more scenes became rendered with all the lighting and textures, more fears were put to bed and even director John Lasseter was floored by the final film.

Though much of the toys are original creations, the film establishes its relatable roots with recognizable and branded toys as secondary characters. Most appear as cameos with the exception of Mr. Potato Head. Thanks to Don Rickles, Potato Head now has an iconic voice and personality. Prior to this film, Potato Head was always recognized as a goofy and silly figure who loved to rearrange his various facial features and body parts. After being shaken and thrown around by Andy's baby sister, Potato Head picks up his parts while grumbling about how he is only approved for ages three and up.

Toy Story has enough character to match its visual achievements, due in part to the wonderful performances. Similar to how Robin Williams was approached for *Aladdin*, animators took Tom Hanks' audio from *Turner and Hooch* and used it for a test animation of Woody. Hanks watched it, thought the voice fit and the rest is history. Tim Allen was another natural fit for Buzz Lightyear, embodying a sense of machismo and heart. Rex (Wallace Shawn) appears as a cheap dinosaur that can't garner a fright and Hamm (John Ratzenberger) appears as the wisecracking piggy bank with some of the best dialogue.

So strong were these characters that they continued on for *Toy Story 2* (1999) and *Toy Story 3* (2010), making for one of the most solid movie trilogies in movie history. It's worth noting that the subsequent sequels went through some rocky roads as *Toy Story 2* was originally going to be a direct-to-video production and *Toy Story 3* was initially going to be animated without Pixar. Thankfully, Pixar restructured these projects and groomed them to be worthy successors that are considered either on par or better than the original movie.

Considering its amazing use of computer graphics, *Toy Story* was nominated for a plethora of accolades from Oscars to Annies. Coupled with its financial success of $361 million worldwide, Walt Disney Pictures became more committed to Pixar producing more CGI features. The original deal was for three animated features, but *Toy Story*'s success expanded that deal to five.

Before the movie had even come out, I was already sold. I'd wait days just to download the trailer in a low-resolution, compressed format from the movie's website. Even at the age of ten, I could sense there was something big to *Toy Story* - a landmark that would open up a new era of filmmaking. Around the same time the movie came out, I became obsessed with Microsoft's 3D Movie Maker software. It was a toy intended for my demographic where pre-rendered characters and animations could be dragged and dropped across a three-dimensional background. Though primitively simple in comparison to Pixar's technology, it was an engrossing piece of software that opened my eyes to computer animation's potential for great storytelling.

Toy Story was very much a toy chest of inspiration. Children saw new toys they could play with, adults saw new technology they could salivate over and filmmakers saw new tools they could use in their future projects. Film critic Roger Ebert theorized on his movie review program that the technique of the film would probably revolutionize animation in the future. He could not have been more right as computer animated films now dominate the theatrical animation landscape of the 21st century. But thanks to the strong characters and writing, *Toy Story* stands tall as more than just the pioneer of the medium. It continues to be just as much an inspiration for filmmaking to shoot for infinity and beyond.

THE TRIPLETS OF BELLEVILLE

Sylvain Chomet's *The Triplets of Belleville* (2003) has this feeling of a dream. It is not a dream of wondrous fantasy or terrifying visions, but something uniquely surreal. There's a sense of familiarity cobbled together from both reality and fantasy. You find yourself spinning out of control in an ever-evolving story that veers off into all sorts of odd directions. By the time you wake up, you're not quite sure what to think, but you find yourself drawn back to such a weird experience.

Even describing the film feels as though I'm trying to relay a dream. A fat little boy lives with his grandmother, Madame Souza, at a crookedly-shaped house in France. The squat grandmother, with her thick glasses and one shoe larger than the other, gently attempts to find something that interests the boy. She tries a piano, a puppy and a train set, but none of it seems to make him happy. Souza eventually strikes gold when she discovers his fondness for bicycles and purchases him a tricycle.

The film then skips ahead a few years and much has changed. The house now shoulders an elevated highway, perfectly level to view passing vehicles from the second floor window. The boy's puppy, Bruno, has grown fat from eating so many leftovers that he can barely stand on his scrawny legs. The pudgy boy has become trimmed and toned as he strives to be an expert cyclist. Madame Souza pushes him to be the best he can be with rigorous exercise, toning of muscles and a strict diet. She goes about this in odd ways, using eggbeaters to stimulate his muscles and having him sit on a scale during dinner that determines how much he should eat. They all appear very content and focused during these scenes as it has become a part of their regular routine, only sharing a smile when they end the night by listening to a record. Though the grownup boy is never given a real name, he is dubbed Champion based on the lettering on the back of his towel.

Champion enters the Tour de France, but is kidnapped by some mysterious men in black suits. Souza, with Bruno in tow, tracks down the kidnappers all the way to Belleville, a metropolis composed of traits from New York City and Montreal. We soon discover that Champion has been captured for the purposes of underground bicycle race gambling. The only hope for Madame Souza finding her boy and defeating the mafia lies in the Triplets of Belleville, a musical trio from the old days that now specialize in improvisational music and battling with frying pans.

Sylvain Chomet has a style wholly original in how he illustrates the characters and their actions. The film opens with a bit of a throwback to 1930's cartoons with its black-and-white picture, rubber-hose animation and satirical caricatures of Josephine Baker and Fred Astaire. We even get a taste of some of the otherworldly humor in which Fred Astaire is eaten by his own shoes and Josephine Baker has her banana skirt ripped apart by horny men turned into monkeys. But when we transition to the present day, or at least further from the 1930's, the world takes on different tones as the characters appear more grotesque in caricature.

Throughout the film, Chomet is constantly breaking animation convention by throwing the story into wild directions not common to commercial animated films. The violence ranges from comical to dark. The nudity ranges from bare breasts to dog genitals. There's even a disgusting riff on Disney when a turd in an unflushed toilet resembles Mickey Mouse. This may make the film seem like a gross-out picture, but there is so much more going on to avoid being just that.

There's an unnatural vibe to just about every character. Champion's torso appears thin as a rail, but his legs are bulging with grossly oversized muscles. The consumerist populace of Belleville is portrayed as overly obese and roundly plump. A small mechanic resembles a mouse with his buck teeth and big ears that all he's missing is the tail. The elderly Triplets hobble along in their long dresses with hunched backs. These designs don't make the characters disgusting, but it doesn't make them cute either. They exist somewhere between extreme exaggeration and uniquely convincing. I especially loved the designs of the gangsters that appear blockish with square shoulders and can blend together when escorting mafia leaders.

Since so many of these characters have compelling designs and mannerisms, they are given their own sequences. With a train rushing by the house every few minutes, Bruno has made it part of his routine to bark at the regularly scheduled train. He later has a strange dream of riding on a train and passing by a house with humans barking at him. In Belleville, we see a lone Triplet sister go fishing for frogs with a grenade. She plops down next to a swamp, tosses the active grenade in the water and eagerly awaits the explosion with a net. The old lady returns home where she feeds her sisters and Souza a feast of frog soup and frozen frogs for desert. These scenes don't advance the story, but they are amusing situations that add to the indescribable atmosphere of the picture.

There is very little dialogue spoken in the film and what little there is present isn't important enough to translate from French to English. The story is entirely told from expression and pantomime. This makes the film both visually creative in its plot and universally humorous. It's easy enough to read the personalities and intentions of all the characters on screen thanks to the flawless character animation. A lanky French waiter of a Belleville restaurant arches his back with his big grin and juts out his arms as he attempts to please his rich customers. No dialogue is required for him as a French-accent of presenting menus and drinks adds nothing to the scene.

Chomet has such a love for traditional hand-drawn animation in how he favors it for this film. He did have to rely on computer graphics for generating some of the denser and more mechanical scenes of cars, bicycles and a roaring sea. Devoted to making his film appear distorted and alive, Chomet was able to make the computer animators add little touches to prevent the CGI from looking too clean or distant from the drawings. While it becomes evident where CGI is used in a few scenes, it never breaks the illusion of Chomet's odd world.

The music, similar to Chomet's drawings, is just as original and unique. The Triplets perform with Madame Souza in a restaurant with their only instruments a newspaper, a fridge grate, a bicycle wheel and a vacuum cleaner. Composer Benoît Charest actually recorded most of these sounds with the household items of the Triplets in the same manner they played them. He recorded the air suction of a vacuum cleaner and placed his fingers over it to get the different whirring sounds of the device.

Chomet's distinct style did not go unnoticed. As his first feature-length animated film, *The Triplets of Belleville* received much critical praise from its festival run and was nominated for two Academy Awards of Best Song and Best Animated Feature (the first PG-13 animated film to be nominated for this category). The acclaim of the picture led to Chomet directing his second animated feature, *The Illusionist* (2010), and guest directing a couch gag for *The Simpsons*.

The originality, energy and detail of *The Triplets of Belleville* make it unlike any other animated film, defying all comparisons. It has a charm, but still has a dark and even cruel edge to its world. It's artistic and character-driven, but not above closing the picture with an exciting car chase of guns and bazookas. Even words such as "surreal" and "odd" can't do it justice. The refusal to be pinned down by any one tone, style or story makes the film a triumph of animation's full potential.

UP

Most animated features aimed at the family tend to feature smart, young prodigies and simple-minded elders. *Up* (2009) flips the script. Here is a grouchy old man with a surprising wealth of ingenuity paired up with a pint-sized boy who is too much of a goof to be the wisest of the pair. The elderly Carl takes center stage as the hero of this adventure through South America. He gripes and mutters as he struggles to keep the innocent Russell alive and well during his expedition.

But the film does not begin with Carl as a bitter old man. We watch the path that led to his current life from his early beginnings. As a young lad, Carl had dreams of exploring the globe for adventure and discovery. He finds an excitable pixie of a girl by the name of Ellie who shares his love for exploration. Carl is very shy when compared to the bouncy Ellie, but she likes him all the more for that trait. Their shared goal is to take a trip to South America. With so much in common, it isn't long before Carl and Ellie get married.

While South America remains in sight, several elements get in the way of that trip. Hospital bills, car bills and home repair bills take their toll on their wallets. A baby was thought to be in the picture, but it does not come to pass. Years go by further and further, the two looking older with each passing scene. Just when it seems that Carl has finally made their lifelong dream come true, Ellie passes away. Carl quietly returns to his house, alone and forlorn.

This entire sequence of events is told in a montage with no dialogue. The music begins fluffy and warm before transitioning to a quieter and tender sound of a lone piano. This was only a few minutes into the film and already the audience I'm seeing this with is drowning in tears. Aside from the boldness of going straight for the emotional jugular right out of the gate, this sequence is the most important part of the movie. It could have been cut out entirely and the movie would still be enjoyable, but having it present creates an unseen level of depth to elderly characters. Carl has lived a long and eventful life of love, joy, sadness and pain. By laying his entire backstory out on the table in such a brisk and heartfelt manner, we're invested a little more in him and his grumpy attitude.

Having established our hero with all our eyes on him, we root for his renewed goal of making it to South America. With no money and his house soon to be destroyed, he puts his skills as a balloon salesman to use by lifting his entire house off the ground with a big batch of colorful balloons. What's causing the sheer force to rip Carl's house off its foundation? It's our need to see him succeed mixed with some of that old Disney wonder.

The original idea for *Up* came from director Pete Docter's fantasies of wanting to escape from all of life's problems. A floating house may not sound the most practical, but it's certainly the most fun. And you can't choose a more secluded destination than the tepui mountains of South America.

Traveling companions pop up along the way in the form of the sweet idiot Boy Scout Russell, a rare bird who Russell names Kevin, and a dog named Doug who speaks his thoughts via a voice-translating collar ("Squirrel!"). They all appear as dopey and walleyed saps that desperately need the help of Carl to survive. Reluctant, but not heartless, he helps them out as it seems to be the right thing to do.

Carl must eventually haul his house on foot towards the peak Ellie once dreamed of living upon. Russell innocently pushes Carl along by talking to the house and saying that Ellie told him they could keep Kevin. Carl looks up at the house to complain ("But I told him no"). It's silly, but emotionally telling of a man who was so accustom to his wife that she remains a character throughout despite never being physically seen on the journey.

The villain out to stop our heroes is a mad explorer by the name of Muntz, a legendary explorer Carl idolized as a child. Obsessed with capturing the mysterious bird known to the group as Kevin, he is a crazy old hermit that has devoted his life to capturing the beast. Any and all visiting explorers were murdered by the crazed adventurer in hopes of acquiring the singular claim to fame. He has secluded himself in his grand airship while his army of dogs patrols the area.

Carl and Muntz share much in common as old men with lifelong goals. Muntz has thrown away most of his life to the hunt and never took the time to enjoy life the way Carl did. Because Muntz represented so much of the dark side that Carl could have been, his ultimate demise became a tricky element for the story department. Various storyboarded endings reveal Muntz being lost forever in a maze of rock, toppling over the edge of a cliff in Carl's house and being launched into the sky by balloons. None of these deaths resonated all that well and carried symbolism that was vague and wrong. Muntz ultimately took the traditional villain exit of falling from a great height.

The South American setting is brilliantly rendered thanks to Pixar's devotion in capturing worlds. Several of the Pixar creative staff traveled to the high elevations of the tepui mountains in the region to gain a sense of the enormity and majesty of it all. After a journey several days long, the animation research team sketched and formed ideas about what to use from the environment for their film. They took note of the strange formation of the rocks which appeared as odd sculptures. These sights came in handy for the optical illusions Carl and Russel experience when finding their way through the clouds and mistaking rocks for people. From touch to temperature to taste, the Pixar team had the total tepui experience.

Another bit of research much closer to home was how to portray the elderly in computer animation. The animators didn't cover Carl in liver spots or have hair coming out his ears, but favored a design that was simpler and more recognizable as an old man. You can spot some obvious inspirations in the face resembling elements of Spencer Tracy and Walter Matthau, but Peter Docter also drew much inspiration from veteran Disney animators. Legendary artist Joe Grant served as the biggest of inspirations as he gave Docter notes and advice on this script before his death in 2005. The influence of these classically trained animators left a lasting impression on Docter as he applied the theme of enjoying the journey of friendship while it lasts. People you love are here one day and gone the next. *Up* reminds us how important it is to relish the days they're here.

Up has a special place in the Pixar pantheon for some major accomplishments. It was the first animated and 3D film ever to open the Cannes Film Festival. It was also the second animated film ever to be nominated for Best Picture at the Academy Awards, the previous being *Beauty and the Beast* (1991). While it did not win, it was rather impressive for the film to receive such a nomination at the same time being nominated for Best Animated Feature, an award which *Up* won without question.

I believe what makes *Up* one of Pixar's greatest achievements is that it's a fine wine. I can see kids enjoying the adorable dog and the goofy kid, but, as they grow older, they'll be able to relate more easily to the emotional journey of Carl. The best animated films are the ones that transcend their demographic - the ones that are just as enjoyable to you as an adult as they were to you as a child. The kids who grow up watching *Up* will have something wonderful to treasure for their later years as the story only improves with age.

WATERSHIP DOWN

The manager of the video store I worked at in high school enforced a rule for only allowing PG-rated movies on the television displays before 9pm. It didn't bother me or my co-workers so much. We'd always go for many of the edgier films released before the PG-13 rating existed. When the manager grew irritated of us always choosing *Gremlins*, *Raiders of the Lost Ark* and *Back to the Future*, she changed the rule to only PG films from the family section. That idea didn't work out so well either as we'd choose more of the pre-PG-13 titles in the family section. Be it the cleavage-heavy fantasy *Wizards* or the expletive-sneaking *Transformers: The Movie*, there was a little something adult in many of the films relegated to the "family" section. When we eventually hit *Watership Down* (1978), she locked us down to Disney movies only, to which we responded with *The Black Hole* and so on.

Though we were essentially goofing off by exploiting loopholes, I'd like to think we were doing a service to the patrons of the video store by revealing these hidden titles of the family section. Somewhere out there is a parent who will unwittingly pick up *Watership Down* for their kids. They won't read the plot synopsis or look up reviews; most of what they'll see is the cute rabbits on the cover and the PG rating. They'll even be duped by the pleasingly playful opening describing the lore of the rabbits. Mom and dad are sure going to feel stupid when a flood of their child's tears follows after witnessing the raw nature of animal brutality and lamenting dialogue of death.

But that is essentially what makes *Watership Down* such a powerful film. It doesn't try to inoculate with overly-cutesy designs or rework the movie into an upbeat musical. The overall serious nature and dark tones of the original novel by Richard Adams are faithfully retained. The rabbits may appear cute, but only in the way they adhere to anatomically correct designs. Their mouths are the only parts exaggerated to allow them to speak in English. Other than some slight comic relief from a seagull voiced by Zero Mostel, the story is played up as a straight adventure. Rabbit Fiver can sense something terrible is coming to the warren in a vision of blood-soaked fields, but the chief won't permit an evacuation. Defying the order of the warren, Fiver teams up with his brother Hazel and a band of rabbit rebels to escape the warren and seek sanctuary elsewhere.

But their path is paved with many horrific dangers. While grazing in an open field, one of the rabbits is snatched up in an instant by a flying predator. A violent trap ensnares one of the rabbits in the throat, forcing him to the ground as he convulses in excruciating pain. One rabbit relays the horrifying experience of being trapped in the burrows, told through terrifying visions of rabbits crammed together in tunnels with exits blocked by suffocated bodies. The ending battle is one of the most terrifyingly gruesome scenes in all of animation as the evil and bloodied Woundwort viciously attacks a warren, biting and scratching his way to victory. This is an animated film that becomes very brutal at times, keeping all the deaths from the original novel and actually adding a few more.

Along with the abundance of violence in the picture, there is a more serious approach to death in coming to terms with it. After Fiver is displaced from Hazel by gun-toting farmers, Fiver follows a vision of the Black Rabbit Inlé, a rabbit grim reaper, which fades in and out as it hops across the fields. While Fiver desperately searches for Hazel, he is haunted by visions of his brother who may or may not be dead when the black rabbit guides him. By the end of the film, Hazel approaches old age and shares a tender conversation with Black Rabbit Inlé about proceeding into the next life. He looks back at his warren of rabbits and accepts his fate by lying down to leave his body behind.

The lore of the picture is amazing in how it doesn't slow down too much to explain the rabbits' sense of community, religion and myth. It can be rather confusing at times trying to keep up with all the terminology, but it's rewarding in that the world of *Watership Down* feels entirely of its own element. This creates a picture that doesn't so much mirror adult themes and allegories as it does utilize them for its own story.

Adding to the emotional tone of the picture is a matching soundtrack by Angela Morley and Malcolm Williamson. Most notable from the soundtrack is Art Garfunkel's "Bright Eyes", an iconic theme song of the picture that went on to become UK's best-selling single of 1979.

The animation style varied throughout the picture with many different styles. The rabbits are traditionally drawn with earth tones while the backgrounds were rendered with watercolors in a variety of hues. The scene of Cowslip's warren stands out as one of the more vivid backgrounds with its use of purple and orange. The prologue is told with a more expressionist style of colors and outlines that contrasts with the more painterly and realistic style of the rest of the picture. Fiver's visions of spirits are simplified to shapes both simple and sketchy as the soul of rabbits spin and split into leafs.

Director Martin Rosen does an exceptional job as a first-time director. He was originally the film's producer while veteran animation artist John Hubley would be the director. But when Hubley died in 1977, Rosen took over directing duties. Some of Hubley's work made it into the film such as the opening prologue. But it was ultimately Rosen that stepped up and gave the film its dark tone that adhered to the book. Some of this can be attributed to the all-star cast of voices that added realism to the characters. John Hurt, Richard Briers, Ralph Richardson and Roy Kinnear all play it straight by not trying to perform cartoon voices. Their performances have a natural grace and add to the serious tone and realism of the picture.

When the film was submitted to the British Board of Film Classification, it surprisingly came back with a rating of 'U', deemed suitable for all ages. The Board reasoned that the movie wouldn't be too troubling for children, but they ended up receiving several complaints over the years for such a rating. I'm not too sure how many complaints the PG rating has received in America given that it wasn't as popular in the US, but I can attest to at least one mother who furiously returned a copy to the video rental store that demanded I give her a refund for traumatizing her children.

Despite the complaints, *Watership Down* was quite the success in the United Kingdom. It did well at the box office, received much critical praise and was nominated for a Hugo Award. The success of the film ultimately led to Martin Rosen directing the similarly toned *The Plague Dogs* (1982), another animated production based on a

Richard Adams novel.

Rosen would additionally serve as executive producer on an animated series for *Watership Down* that ran on British television from 1999 to 2001. With 39 episodes, the series diverged greatly from both the novel and the film with the addition of new storylines, characters and warrens. Some elements from the film were carried over such as a new rendition of "Bright Eyes" and the returning voices of John Hurt and Richard Briers (though they didn't voice the same characters they played in the original film).

While I joke about *Watership Down* not being for young children, it is perhaps best suited for older children entering their teen years. Director Guillermo del Toro remembers watching the film at such an age and dubbed it as a rite of passage for an animation that dealt with more adult themes. At an age when cartoons and animated films start being labeled in the schoolyard as kid's stuff, *Watership Down* reveals that animation can be capable of more than fairytales and comedy. A story about rabbits does not have to be cute and gentle - it can be dark and adult with themes of spirituality, environmentalism and rebellion. Disney this was not.

WHEN THE WIND BLOWS

Everyone has their favorite animated film that's so sad it always makes them cry. It may be *Bambi* for the heartbreaking off-screen death of the titular deer's mother. It could be *Watership Down* for how such cute creatures as rabbits would be bloodied and ripped to shreds by each other. Personally, nothing generates more sadness than *When the Wind Blows* (1986). What separates it from the competition is its lack of hope. There is no way out for this chipper old English couple. They are doomed from the first act and there isn't a single thing they can do to prevent their tragic fate from unfolding with grim results. What's so depressing is that they themselves don't realize their lives are ending very soon. Or perhaps they do as they attempt to keep stiff upper lips throughout.

Reflecting the Cold War era, an elderly English couple living in Sussex prepare for the event of an atomic bomb explosion. James and Hilda gently prattle on about the olden days as they take the recommended precautions for doomsday. The pamphlets they read offer them worthless advice for survival such as fastening a door to a wall to create your very own radiation bunker. But the couple still trusts the government in that everything will be okay. They don't seem too worried as they continue making small talk during preparations about their adult son living in the city and what they should do with the rest of their day.

And then it happens. An atomic bomb goes off miles away from their cottage home. They hunker down in their "shelter" and wait out the initial aftermath. As the bomb decimates the surrounding countryside, there are flashbacks on the early lives of James and Hilda. Such imagery amid sketched scenes of cars toppling and homes crumbling gives the impression that they have died. In one sense, they already have. Though they survive the blast, the resulting fallout has sealed their fate.

There's an uncomfortable ambivalence to the couple's perceptions on nuclear holocaust. When James initially returns from the public library with the pamphlets to relay the current news about nuclear war, Hilda brushes off such topics with mild concern. James doesn't seem that worried either given his high faith in the government. With his age and experience having lived through one war, he believes a new threat can't possibly be as terrible. The government would be prepared and knowledgeable enough to deliver proper survival techniques, he rationalizes. Hilda even talks about her diplomatic tactics of sending a letter to the Soviets to politely ask them not to drop any bombs.

Even as James prepares the make-shift fallout shelter, the couple still approaches the subject with a casual nature. Hilda seems more concerned with the shelter damaging the wallpaper than actually protecting them against radiation. The prospect of spending 14 days in such a space with an alternative means of a toilet disgusts her even more than dying of radiation. But such fears do not exist in her mind or even James'. They haven't been briefed on such atrocities and are not prepared for them. The effects of the radiation making them lose their hair and change the color of their skin are rationalized as a part of getting older.

Their ignorance leads them to several stupid mistakes on how to act after a nuclear bomb has been dropped. The couple gathers rainwater from outside for a drink, unaware of the fallout that has contaminated it so. Their reasoning is that fallout must be something they can see as if it were a visible gas that attacks humans. They are completely clueless about what is slowly killing them. The soundtrack becomes a character as well the way it signifies their fatal mistakes.

But what makes the film truly sad is that we actually care about this couple. They're oblivious to the true effects of an atomic bomb due to inept government information, but only in being as trustworthy and calm as a kindly old couple can be. The sunny countryside has provided them with a sense of peace and easygoing that is hard to abandon when war is presented. It brings more humanity and perspective to their situation which makes it harder to be enraged at their mistakes.

Decades before this film was released, there were short animated films advising children and families about how to handle an atomic blast. The prime suggestion was to duck and cover as a cartoon illustrates that organic life is perfectly fine if they lower themselves and form a shield with their arms. Many years after those shorts, we have a film that illustrates the fruitless results of such preparations. The animated elderly couple do not prop themselves up and walk away unscathed. They believe they are just as fine as the cartoon characters from the short films, but we know they are not long for this world.

The film is anti-government, but not very political, in how it displays what happens when those that cling without question to the word of superiors are left out to dry. After the bomb explodes, James and Hilda are under the impression that British forces will arrive to provide relief. They never come. There are no radio signals to find or any passing planes or automobiles to spot. The couple is on their own and continue to operate under the illusion that help is just a day or two away. What's most intriguing about watching this picture is trying to decipher just when the two come to terms with their own demise. How long do they go along with their mindset until they're just forcing themselves to go through the motions of being brave? We see the weariness on their faces as they slowly decay, but never see them give up as they continue to wallow in denial.

This was the first animated film to be directed by Jimmy Murakami, previously a supervising director on the animated adaptation of Raymond Briggs' *The Snowman* (1982). Prior to these two films, Murakami had a long history of creating short animated films, including a segment for the adult animated feature *Heavy Metal* (1981). It took six months for Murakami to adapt the original graphic novel into a completed storyboard for a feature film. He originally wanted to use American animators because he thought they'd be able to better deliver the film he wanted, but was convinced to use British animators that more than met the challenge.

The animation found different ways to be experimental. During the scenes in and around the home, the characters are traditionally drawn while the backgrounds are three-dimensional sets. Model sets were built for the backgrounds in which the camera could track and pan around the house with cel animation layered on top of the footage. The model of the house was so detailed and intricate that you'd swear it was built for a stop-motion film. The effect becomes creepier towards the end as the couple slowly disappears from the setting, quietly slipping into their safety suits that are actually garbage bags. Filming of the built sets took ten weeks.

The scenes of destruction and memories are perceived more in a sketchy line-art fashion, appearing more dreamlike and nightmarish with varying tones. Live-action footage of missile carriers and army equipment was inserted early in the picture to orient the viewer on the reality of the setting. In addition, live-action footage of model rockets, submarines and airplanes were shot to convey a sense of doom that was a little closer to the style of the animation. Worth noting is that the first bit of live-action footage shot for the production was reference of people using the makeshift shelter depicted in the film.

The characters of James and Hilda were voiced by veteran actors Peggy Ashcroft and John Mills. Neither of them had voiced animated characters before. Despite never having experience with animation, their performances are very natural and match the meticulously graceful character animation well. Ashcroft and Mills were recorded for three days and were apparently quite professional - the last nine minutes of dialogue in the film was all completed in one take.

Perhaps the most surprising aspect of the production is the soundtrack. The title song is an original piece sung by David Bowie – a bittersweet melody to close the picture. There are also additional pieces from other top talents that include Genesis and Paul Hardcastle. The majority of the music was composed by Roger Waters.

When the Wind Blows is a story that could easily be adapted to a stage play for its simple setting and premise. But the limitless potential of animation allows the original graphic novel to breathe with more horror and surrealism to the topic of nuclear fallout. It's surprisingly engaging for being overly talky thanks to Murakami's unique direction and Briggs' well-written dialogue. The powerful visuals give the viewer moments to identify with James and Hilda in how they treasure the past and avoid facing their mortality. The last few moments as the couple wither and pray for everything to be okay is one of the most moving and terrifying scenes I've ever seen in any animated film. It's a chilling reminder of how ill-prepared we all are for the end - be it an atomic bomb or old age.

WHO FRAMED ROGER RABBIT

Who Framed Roger Rabbit (1988) is a rather historic animated feature for its many groundbreaking achievements. It's the first time hand-drawn animation actually crossed over live-action with so many minute details to make a seamless blending of dimensions. It's the first film with cartoon characters to present a noir detective story that's played mostly straight in between all the cartoony visuals. But most noteworthy is that for once the barriers of Warner Brothers and Disney were broken. Donald Duck and Daffy Duck bicker at each other over dueling pianos. Mickey Mouse and Bugs Bunny have a mid-air conversation about parachutes. Such sights are both a marvel and a rarity of so many cartoon characters trading wits. The good news is that if the gimmick wears off, the film itself is still a darn good story with some impressive technical skill behind it.

In the 1940's Hollywood setting, cartoon characters exist as real entities sharing the same dimension and studios with live-action actors. The toons originate from Toontown, their two-dimensional home with its bordering wall just outside town. Most of these living drawings work as actors in shorts for the Maroon Cartoon studio. Its owner is R.K. Maroon, a man who is quite pleased with such deals as landing a contract with Dumbo working for peanuts. Other characters fulfill jobs as either nightclub entertainers or hired muscle. These colorful characters capable of all forms of comedy in our world are mostly accepted by society.

Detective Eddie Valiant (Bob Hoskins) despises the toons, however, after one of them killed his brother by dropping an anvil on his head. The silly slapstick logic of cartoons does not apply to humans. One cartoon character's flattening gag is another human's untimely death. Drowning in booze and debt, Eddie is reluctant to take on his latest case with investigating a possible affair of toon wife Jessica Rabbit cheating on her cartoon rabbit husband, Roger Rabbit.

His trail leads him to a secret club where Jessica performs as a stage singer. Eddie snags a seat and receives a drink from his old acquaintance Betty Boop, working as a waitress after color pictures destroyed her black-and-white career. As an interesting parallel between cartoons and reality, Betty is voiced by the original Mae Questel who hadn't performed as the character in fifty years. When Jessica finally hits the stage, the film achieves its most mesmerizing scene and not just because a buxom lounge singer was animated so sexually.

Watch how Jessica, a hand-drawn creation, moves through the audience of live-action actors. She picks up hats, squeezes cheeks and pulls on ties. The camera follows her around the club as the stage lights make her dress shimmer and her body cast shadows. There are no visible strings or kinks in the technical process for this sequence. You completely buy that cartoon characters co-exist with three-dimensional beings.

The plot Eddie uncovers manages to be both silly and dark. He snaps a few photos of Jessica having an affair with the head of the ACME Corporation, but their secret fun amounts to a literal game of patty-cake. Such news makes the wild Roger Rabbit become depressed and furious, sobbing a mess until a shot of booze sends him bouncing off the walls with rage. Soon after the case, the head of ACME is crushed to death under a crate and all eyes are on Roger who seeks Eddie's help in clearing his name.

Bob Hoskins as Eddie helped establish the foundation for actors working with cartoon characters. There are already enough antics going on in the picture with all sorts of cartoons bouncing around and causing mischief. The best way to act in this scenario is to play it straight which Hoskins does with gusto. He's playing a real detective and not a detective inside a cartoon. This type of acting was carried over into similar feature films where it worked exceptionally well for Michael Jordan (*Space Jam*) and Brendan Fraser (*Looney Tunes: Back in Action*).

If the technical achievements don't seem apparent for some viewers, you need only compare it to another animation/live-action hybrid, *Cool World* (1992). Both movies featured detectives, a town of toons and lots of interaction between the two dimensions. But take a look at *Cool World* when Brad Pitt's character attempts to wrap his arm around his cartoon dame. Notice how awkward and out of place he appears with his hand hovering around her shoulder. You can see the strings of an actor working against nothing. Compare that to the scenes in *Roger Rabbit* with Jessica Rabbit pushing and pulling at Eddie's clothes. It's far more convincing for nailing the smallest of details as a combination of the actor, the director, the effects technicians and the animators.

Take note in *Cool World* how all over the place the world of cartoon characters appear. The screen seems to randomly splatter various drawings around, feeling more as if somebody is drawing over the picture rather than adding to it. The only scene where the drawings interacting with the live-action characters seem effective is with Kim Basinger's character. This is a bit of a cheat, however, since she is entirely rotoscoped - Kim was filmed in live-action and traced over by animators. It's much easier to create the illusion of meeting dimensions when there is something real to work off of.

For *Who Framed Roger Rabbit*, however, director Robert Zemeckis uses plenty of tricks to make all the animation melding believable. A thin robotic arm was used for scenes where animated characters would interact with live-action as when Roger smashes plates on his head and Baby Herman holds a cigar. A modified go-kart was used for when Eddie rides on Benny, the cartoon cab. Hoskins sat on top with a steering wheel while a driver below maneuvered the go-kart at 40 miles per hour. Even basic puppetry was used for the cartoon penguins serving drinks at a club. Rubber puppets were used as reference points for the live-action actors working with cartoon characters, but the final shots were mostly the actors performing pantomime. Bob Hoskins described the experience as acting with ghosts.

There's a certain magic in which the viewer is left perplexed at how the filmmakers were able to plan out such scenes. Eddie holds Roger under the water of his kitchen sink, pretending to do his laundry, while cartoon henchmen search his apartment. One of the goons makes a parting threat to Eddie in which he lightly splashes the water of the sink. After they depart, Roger bursts from the sink in a violent explosion of water and gives Eddie a big smooch in thanks. I absolutely love this scene just trying to decipher how every little action was planned and implemented.

While still showcasing the classic cartoon traits of Warner Brothers and Disney, the story had a rawer noir angle. When there aren't madcap antics happening on screen, the story becomes rather dark. One of the most terrifying moments for the younger viewers came when Eddie finally discovers the identity of the murderer. The suspect is a cartoon character masquerading in a human appearance. He removes his three-dimensional eyes to reveal big and buggy cartoon eyes. His voice grows higher and more menacing. His arms transform into sharp cartoon weapons that he uses to attack Eddie. His insanity as a murderous cartoon character is rather frightening right up to his gruesome death with him screaming all the way to the toon afterlife.

As with any Disney animated picture, there was a controversy in the visuals. But unlike the instances in *The Little Mermaid* or *The Lion King* which were unintentional, *Roger Rabbit's* adult Easter egg seemed much more on purpose. In a scene where Jessica Rabbit is thrown from Benny the cab, her landing reveals in one frame that she is not wearing underwear. When this controversy hit the news, there was a surge in sales of the Laserdisc edition which allowed for better quality and an easier method of going frame-by-frame. Disney altered this scene for future releases to not feature animated nudity. It's hard to say if leaving it in would have caused a surge in DVD sales. One amusing Easter egg that still remains is with the cartoon train that zooms across the screen in the finale. Freeze those shots and you'll see a different murder in every train car.

Who Framed Roger Rabbit was a big box office success in that it grossed $328 million worldwide. Despite such success, a sequel was not immediately produced. It's understandable considering how expensive it was to achieve such results of blending animation and live-action. The original cartoon characters of the movie, however, did go on to star in three short animated films. There were plans for a prequel that was in development since the 1990's, but that has yet to solidify as of this writing.

Film critic Gene Siskel remarked that he almost didn't want to know how the special effects were done for *Roger Rabbit* to still be amazed on repeat viewings. Perhaps that's what makes the film so genius. Its premise entertains the idea that cartoons do not exist as paper creations, but real characters that can stand alongside real actors. The idea matches the logic of a child's vision on cartoons, but this film lets the adults buy into that sense of magic as well.

YELLOW SUBMARINE

By the late 1960's, The Beatles were burnt out on movie and television projects. *A Hard Day's Night* (1964) and *Help!* (1965) proved too tiring for the musical foursome and their animated TV series was a disappointment to them. So when an animated movie popped up on their contract with United Artists, the musical group distanced themselves from the project. They provided music for the film, but did not voice their own characters as they were far busier with their music projects. It was intended to be their last film with United Artists, but the lack of The Beatles in the cast ultimately led to *Let It Be* (1970) being the final film on their contract.

Upon visiting the studio during production, however, The Beatles were astonished to find that *Yellow Submarine* (1968) was actually brilliant on a visual and storytelling level. Though it was too late for The Beatles to provide their own voices at that point in production, the band was filmed in a live-action sequence that ended the picture. It's tacked on and doesn't match with the animation given their altered appearances compared to the character designs, but it still gives the picture a Beatles seal of approval that felt genuine more than contractual (though they apparently were supposed to appear in the picture at some point under the contract).

Due to the lateness of The Beatles to the project, *Yellow Submarine* was an ever-evolving production over the course of eleven months that was assembled as it went. The script and the art were being developed at the same time which led to the rather lucid story structure. The basics of the story are simple enough for a fantasy film built around the popularity of a music group. The wondrous Pepperland is under attack by the negative forces of the Blue Meanies. So contrarian that they forbid "yes" from their vocabulary, the Meanies remove music and pleasure from Pepperland. Old Fred escapes in a yellow submarine and travels to Liverpool where he enlists the aid of The Beatles. Their power of music saves day.

Written by four collaborators, one of which being Erich Segal of *Love Story* fame, the script had a strangely freeform quality in how it approached the dialogue. The Beatles' were kept charismatic throughout by mostly making puns and jokes as if they were more witty poets than musicians. To incorporate many of The Beatles' songs into the picture, the story was kept very loose with several stops for musical numbers. They become lost in the Foothills of Headlands and sing "Lucy in the Sky with Diamonds" while walking through the arrays of colorfully filled heads. While in the Sea of Nothing, The Beatles happen upon a strange clown figure in which they start singing about him as the "Nowhere Man". It was a format echoing that of *Fantasia* as a music video showcase that would carry on into similar films such as Pink Floyd's *The Wall*.

Because of its segmented approach, *Yellow Submarine* is best remembered in moments rather than its overall story. The varied style of each scene differs greatly from the other and keeps a high level of interest throughout. Live-action footage was sketched over and splashed with shifting colors for the Foothills of the Headlands scene. Gradiant changes in color gave a more trippy sense of shifting reality. Perspective is toyed with when the group enters the Sea of Holes, unsure of which hole goes up or down.

The film's visual style was envisioned by art director Heinz Edelmann who portrayed The Beatles with painterly abstraction. He had limited material to work with, relying mostly on the pictures of The Beatles from their album covers to create their design. With disproportionate bodies and a flat style, Edelmann's designs were perfectly suited to match the psychedelic nature of The Beatles' music.

Whereas Disney animation strived for fluidity and a sense of realism, *Yellow Submarine* made great use of its limited animation by favoring color and staging. The various worlds that lead to Pepperland are a treat for the eyes where anything and everything can happen. Time can be sped up or slowed down, dimensions can be crossed and soundwaves can be seen next to colorful interpretations of the characters.

Though the film was a major hit in Europe, the ending was altered for the American release for fear of the film being too long for American audiences. The original ending featured the song "Hey Bulldog" during a battle sequence, but director Al Brodax cut this scene and replaced it with new animation of the ending battle. The scene was eventually added back in for the 1999 home video release.

Yellow Submarine opened the gates for a new breed of animated cinema. Animation was no longer bound by the common constraints of attempting to be lovable and huggable for the family audience. It was a medium that could be psychedelic, surreal and adult. By the 1970's, more animated films followed that pushed the boundaries of both style and content - from the trippy sci-fi setting of *Fantastic Planet* to the irreverently crude nature of *Fritz the Cat*.

There's no doubt that the broad success of the picture was due to the involvement of The Beatles, but it's surprising how little of their involvement makes the picture shine. Though The Beatles didn't voice their own characters, the cast chosen mesh well into the roles of the iconic four. Much of the animation team appeared in the live-action footage that was used for a variety of the animation sequences. Heinz Edelmann thinks of the film as a sort of biography of everyone who worked on it in addition to being a documentary of the 1960's.

Surprisingly, the film has gone through spats of being out of print. The film negatives were damaged over the years from dust, dirt and scratches which gave MGM plenty to do for the 1999 video restoration. Despite being considered a dated period piece by the copyright holders, *Yellow Submarine* remains as timeless as The Beatles music. It was definitive proof that you don't need the latest technology, the biggest budget or an adherence to the norm to be an animation classic. All you need is love, some talented artists and The Beatles.

ABOUT THE AUTHOR

Mark McPherson has written as a professional film critic for MovieSpoon.com and has a Bachelor of Science in Media Arts and Animation. He lives and works in St. Louis Park, Minnesota.

MadnessMark.com

Made in the USA
Middletown, DE
25 September 2016